RUNES AND THE ORIGINS OF WRITING

ALAIN DE BENOIST

RUNES
AND THE ORIGINS OF WRITING

ARKTOS
LONDON 2018

Copyright © 2018 by Arktos Media Ltd.

All rights reserved. No part of this book may be reproduced or utilized in any form or by any means (whether electronic or mechanical), including photocopying, recording or by any information storage and retrieval system, without permission in writing from the publisher.

Printed in the United Kingdom.

ISBN	978-1-912079-11-7 (Print)
	978-1-912079-10-0 (Ebook)
TRANSLATION	Jean Bernard
EDITING	Martin Locker and Melissa Mészáros
DESIGN	Tor Westman

Arktos.com   fb.com/Arktos   @arktosmedia   arktosmedia

CONTENTS

PART I

Writing and Oral Tradition. 1
Runic Writing. 4
The Characteristics of *Fuþark*. 6
Runic Inscriptions 10
The Oldest Inscriptions 12
Inscriptions on Wood. 16
The Origin Issue 20
The Latin Theory 23
The Greek Theory 29
The North Italic Theory 32
The Contribution of Linguistics 38
Provisional Appraisal 44

PART II

Attempts at Explanation 60
Symbols and "Pre-Writings" 65
The Debate On "Magic" 69
The Word "Rune" 76
Divination and Oracular Use 79
"Magic" Vocabulary 84
Óðinn and the "Divine Origin" of the Runes 87
Runic Magic in Sagas — The Runesmith 92

PART III

The Three Phases of the Moon 98
Eight and Nine 106
The Norns, the Parcae and the Moirai. 111
The Homology Between Day and Year 114
The Rune for The Word "Year" 118
Asterisms and Constellations 120

PART IV

"Phoinika Grammata" 133
From the Phoenicians to the Greeks 135
Before the Phoenicians 140
The Phoenician Alphabet 144
The Sea Peoples 148
From the Philistines to the Phoenicians 152
The Etruscans 156
From Etruscan to Latin 161

Index 165

NOTE. The abbreviations used in this books are conform to ordinary usage. The asterisk [*] before some words means that they are terms reconstructed by linguists that do not have a written confirmation.

Dedicated to François-Xavier Dillmann.

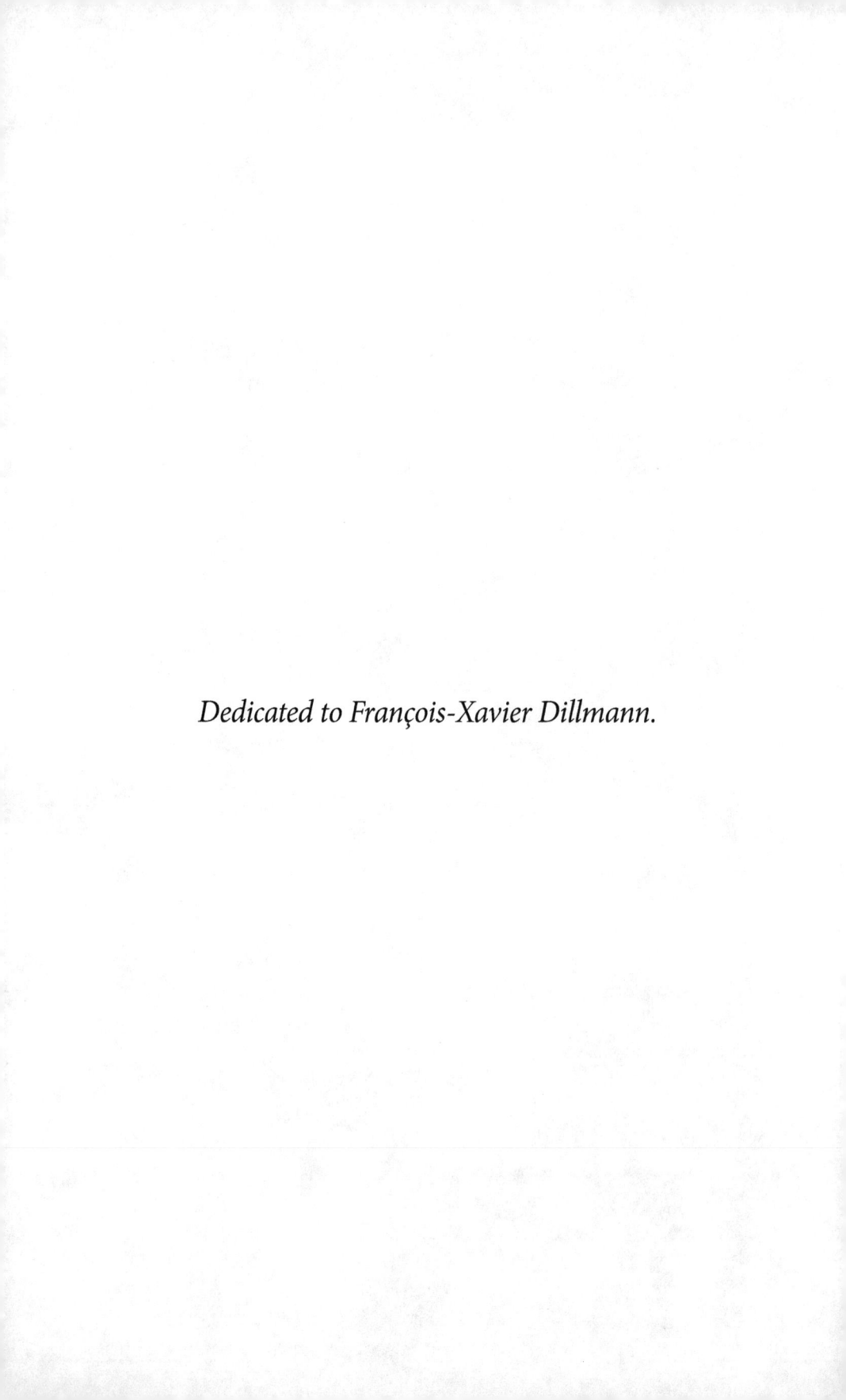

PART I

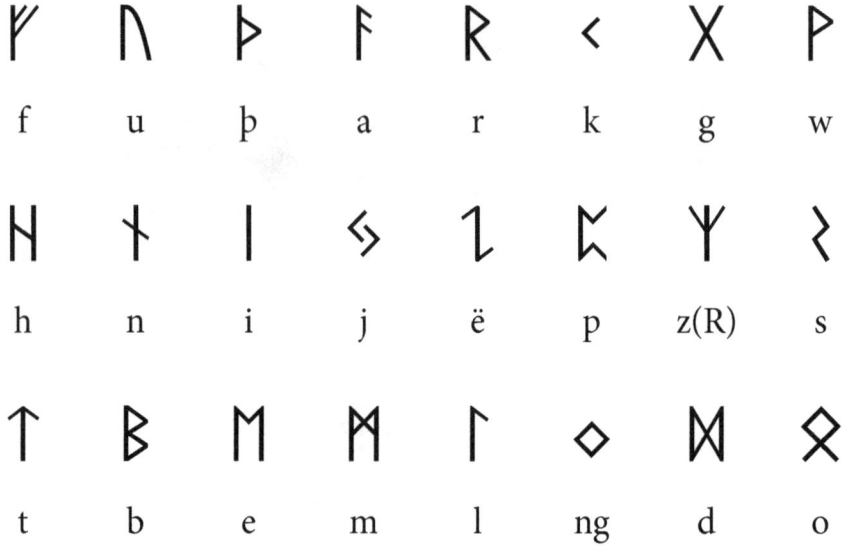

THE OLDER runic "alphabet" (*Fuþark*),
comprising twenty-four letters grouped into three "ættir."

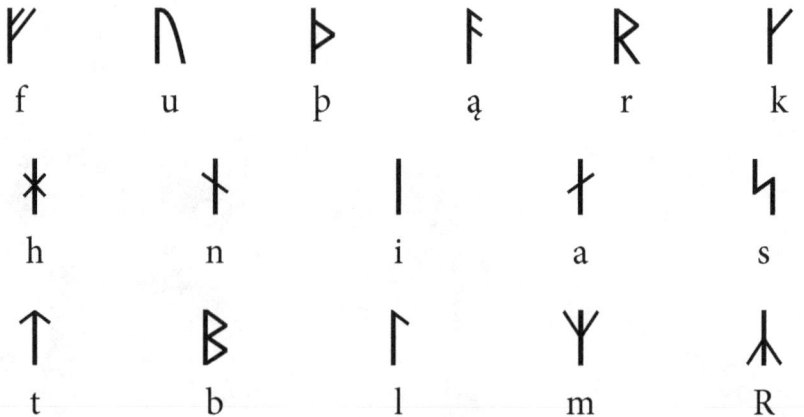

THE MODERN *Fuþark*, 16 letters.

1

Writing and Oral Tradition

"Any conception of culture that would designate the propensity to write as an indicator of a culture's wealth and complexity should be discarded," writes Eric A. Havelock. "A culture can rely entirely on some kind of spoken communication and nevertheless be a culture with all that it entails."[1]

That preliminary remark is useful in understanding why there is no common Indo-European term to refer to writing, in spite of the early development of several writing systems by ancient Near-Eastern cultures for administrative and utilitarian purposes. The Indo-European tradition is indeed essentially oral, and most Indo-European people seem to have voluntarily ignored writing, in its contemporary sense. Bernard Sergent describes that "singular phenomenon" as follows:

> Writing is not categorically *rejected*, but it is put to the side to prioritize orality which comes first and foremost. In *all* ancient Indo-European cultures, or almost all of them, there is that rejection or marginalization, its use is very specific. It is that way because writing has an ambiguous status: on the one hand it has cons, written culture is perceived by those people to be of inferior quality compared to spoken culture [...] but on the other hand it has pros, as writing is also perceived to be somewhat magical because it makes things last and popularizes them.[2]

---

[1] Eric A. Havelock, *Aux origines de la civilisation écrite en Occident*, François Maspéro, Paris 1981, p. 12.

[2] Bernard Sergent, *Les Indo-Européens. Histoire, langues, mythes*, Payot, Paris 1995, p. 386.

It is worth remembering that last point.

That is why writing plays no part in Vedic religion. The Brahmins' role is to preserve the Vedas by reciting the text and learning it by heart to keep the oral transmission going. The sacred scriptures of the Indo-Aryan culture are a revelation confided to the ear, literally a "hearing" (*shruti*). While the Brahmin tradition exalts the strength of the spoken word (the very name of the Brahmins comes from *bráhman* "poetic spell"), it neglects scriptural activities, but it does not mean that they are ignored. In the Veda language, there is no verbal root for "the act of writing." In the Sanskrit vocabulary, the term for "letter" (verna) originally meant a kind of sound, it was a phonetics term. The earliest Sanskrit manuscripts only date from the 5th century [Editor's Note: All dates are AD unless specified], with their Asoka chancellery inscriptions. The Vedas, which have been transmitted orally for at least 4000 years, have only been written down in the 18th century.

In Iran, the *Avesta* had also only been written down in the Sassanid period. The Celts shared the druidic teachings exclusively orally (this is why there are no remains of it). Arbois de Jubainville writes about druids from Gaul that "we know that their teaching comprised making their students learn by heart a long didactic poem that they sang and that was actually memorized correctly by some students only after twenty years of studying."[3] Cesar also emphasized the hostility which druids showed when they were told to write down their knowledge:

> novice druids learned a lot of verses; many of them study for over twenty years; they don't think their religion allows the writing down of verses (*neque fas esse existimant eas litteris mandare*) but they do use Greek letters for all kinds of public and private uses.[4]

Christian J. Guyonvarc'h, according to whom the conversion to Christianism implied a conversion to the written tradition, tells us that "there are no native words in any Celtic language for the act of writing or reading."[5] He adds that there is no ancient Celtic epigraphy for the

---

3   Henry d'Arbois de Jubainville, *Les druides et les dieux celtiques à forme d'animaux*, Honoré Champion, Paris 1906.

4   Caesar, *De bello gallico*, 1, VI, c. 14, § 3.

5   Christian J. Guyonvarc'h, "La conversion de l'Irlande au christianisme et à l'écriture," in *Connaissance des religions*, June 1990, p. 22. See also Georges Dumézil, "La tradition

regions far from the Mediterranean, as well as no writings in Gaulish in north-eastern Gaul. The Celtic name for writing (Old-Irish: *scrib-*) comes from Latin *scribo*. In Scandinavia, the skalds' art had also been transmitted orally for a long time.

Plutarch said about Numa that, according to him, "it was wrong to preserve religious secrets in inanimate letters," which explains why he was thought to be the father of an "'unwritten tradition' by Rome."[6] So too thought Pythagoras ("religious secrets should not be entrusted to inert things") and Lycurgus, the legendary lawgiver of Sparta, who made never the writing of laws a constitutional principle.[7]

The importance of oral tradition must be kept in mind when one delves into writing.

---

druidique et l'écriture: le vivant et le mort," in Jacques Bonnet (ed.), *Georges Dumézil*, Pandora/Centre Georges Pompidou, Paris 1981, pp. 325–338.

6 *Life of Numa*, XXII, 2.
7 *Lycurgus*, XIII, 1–2.

2

Runic Writing

RUNIC WRITING IS THE WRITING SYSTEM that was used to transcribe different Germanic languages before the Latin script, and then alongside it. It seems to have appeared roughly in the 1st century AD and it was still used up to the 14th century, when it began to fall out of use. However, it was still used marginally in the 17th and 18th centuries in some parts of the Swedish and Norwegian countryside (Dalarna, Härjedalen, Telemark, Gotland, etc.) Its oldest variety comprises twenty-four signs or runes which form an "alphabet" which was given the name *Fuþark* ("Futhark") because of its particular order. Those twenty-four runes, materialized by vertical or oblique strokes, transcribe twenty-four sounds or phonemes. The *Fuþark* comprises eighteen consonants and six vowels. Runes in the available body of inscriptions manifest a striking unity. Most of them are almost always the same; there are only minor variations and they rarely are isolated.

The former *Fuþark* that had twenty-four signs stopped being used in the 8th century. A new *Fuþark* reduced to sixteen signs appeared in the beginning of the 9th century in the Danish isles and in southern Sweden.[1] That was the one used in the so-called Viking era. We know of three main varia-

---

[1] Wilhelm Grimm (1786–1859), who was one of the precursors of scientific runology (*Über die deutsche Runen*, Dieterich, Göttingen 1821) still thought that the sixteen sign *Fuþark* was the oldest one. That theory has been dropped for a long time now. Jakob Hornemann Bredstorff (1790–1841), followed by Ludwig F. A. Wimmer (1839–1929), was the first one to demonstrate as early as 1822 that the sixteen sign *Fuþark* is but a transformation of the original twenty-four rune *Fuþark*.

tions: the "long stroke runes," the "short stroke runes" and the "Norwegian (ancient) runes." The transition from the old to the new sixteen-rune *Fuþark* is one of the most talked about issues of runology.[2] Did it happen through a voluntary reform or was it rather a progressive evolution? Some specialists simply don't believe that the new *Fuþark* comes from the old. Some others accept the derivation but they explain it through other means. There's a disagreement between the upholders of the "utilitarian" hypothesis and those of the strictly linguistic theory. The former think that the "reform" comes strictly from a wish to simplify, which is quite dubious; the latter claim that it is the result of phonetic disruptions that affected the Proto-Scandinavian system. Lastly, some suggest (without any precise argument) a desire to make the *Fuþark* more incomprehensible in the age of the first Christian missions. René L. M. Derolez writes that

> that reform could not have been introduced for practical purposes: reading the new alphabet is much harder than reading the old one, because many sounds can't be expressed accurately by the new one. It may be a reaction against Christianism, which was making an entrance at the boundaries of Scandinavia. It was precisely when Charlemagne got his armies to the borders of Denmark. That pending danger could have provoked a revival of the pagan culture.[3]

Since we are studying the origins of runic writing, we are only interested in the Old *Fuþark*, not the sixteen signs one nor the other runic writing systems that were confirmed later on, like the twenty-eight sign Anglo-Saxon *Fuþorc* that was developed in the British Isles after the Angles, Jutes and Saxons' invasion, the Frisian system, the *Fuþorc* used around 800 in Northumbria and in north-western England, the pointed runes, the Rök runes, the Hälsingland runes, the medieval *Fuþark*, etc.

---

2   See Aslak Liestøl, "The Viking Runes: The Transition from the Older to the Younger 'Fuþark'," in *Saga-Book*, 20/4, University College, London 1981, pp. 247–266; Michael Schulte, "The Transformation of the Older *Fuþark*: Number Magic, Runographic or Linguistic Principles," in *Arkiv för nordisk filologi*, 2006, pp. 41–74; Michael Schulte, "Neue Überlegungen zum Aufkommen des jüngeren Fuþarks," in *Beiträge zur Geschichte der deutschen Sprache und Literatur*, 2009, pp. 229–251; Michael Schulte, "Der Problemkreis der Übergangsinschriften im Lichte neuerer Forschungbeiträge," in John Ole Askedal et al. (Hg.), *Zentrale Probleme bei der Erforschung der älteren Runen. Akten einer internationalen Tagung an der Norwegischen Akademie der Wissenschaft*, Peter Lang, Frankfurt/M. 2010, pp. 163–189; Michael P. Barnes, "Phonological and Graphological Aspects of the Transitional Inscriptions," ibid., pp. 191–207.

3   René L. M. Derolez, *Les dieux et la religion des Germains*, Payot, Paris 1962, p. 175.

3

The Characteristics of *Fuþark*

COMPARED TO OTHER WRITINGS from western Europe, runic writing has some notable features that must be taken into account to determine its origins. The first one is the order of the letters within the "alphabet." *Fuþark* is called *Fuþark* because its first letters are f, u, þ (th), a, r, k, then g, w, n, i, j, ï, p, z (or R), s, t, b, e, m, l, ŋ (ng), d and o. So, the order is totally different from the order of Mediterranean alphabets. Specialists notice it but seldom try to explain it. "There is no theory that has ever been put out that can satisfy the needs of linguists when it comes to explaining why the Germans chose that particular sequence," explains Terje Spurkland.[1]

Fifteen runic inscriptions give us all or almost all of the *Fuþark* in its canonical order. Almost all of them date back to the 5th or 6th century. The oldest one is the one from the Kylver stone, found in 1903 in its tomb in Gotland, which seems to date back to the beginning of the 5th century (c. 400). The Grumpan bracteate (c. 475–500), found in 1911 in Västergötland, gives us a complete *Fuþark* that is two letters short of being identical to that found on the Kylver stone. Another Swedish bracteate, the Vadstena bracteate (c. 550), found in 1774 in Östergötland, bears a similar sequence but it reads from right to left starting at the support hole, whereas the Grumpan

---

1 Terje Spurkland, *Norwegian Runes and Runic Inscriptions*, Boydell Press, Woodbridge 2005, pp. 5–6.

bracteate reads from left to right. The fibula of Charnay (Saône-et-Loire), found in 1858 and dating back to c. 580, bears an incomplete *Fuþark* for lack of space. The fibula with golden silver from Aquincum in Hungary (c. 500) gives us the first eight runes. There is also the inscription (c. 535) discovered in 1930 on a marble column of a Byzantine church from Breza, twenty-two kilometers northwest of Sarajevo, the Beuchte fibula found near Goslar, the Lindkær bracteate (Denmark), etc.

Another very important characteristic — probably the most important — is the division of *Fuþark* letters. Runes don't form a continuous sequence like the Greek or Latin scripts, but they are grouped together into three eight-letter long immutable sequences (From ᚠ to ᚹ, from ᚻ to ᛋ, from ᛏ to ᛟ). That is confirmed by the bracteates of Grumpan and Vadstena. They show the complete *Fuþark* sequence divided up into three eight-letter groups, separated by six lined-up dots (Grumpan) or two dots, one on top of the other (Vadstena). Those three runic sequences are called *ættir* (singular *ætt*). That denomination can be found in a 17th century Icelandic text, but also in an 11th century manuscript (*Isruna-Traktat*). That term, which means "a whole made of eight parts," is a *ti- derivative from *ahta which means "eight" in German (see Old High German *ahti-* "eight," Old Norse *átta*, same meaning). The fact that it is a homophone with *ætt* "family" (*geschlecht*) seems fortuitous: *ætt comes from *aih-ti which means "property" in German, and its verbal basis is *aih* "I own" (see *aihts* in Gothic). In Icelandic manuscripts from the 17th century, every *ætt* is under the authority of a god: Freyr (*Frøys ætt*, which begins with the ᚠ = f rune), Heimdallr (*Hagals ætt*, which begins with the ᚻ = h rune) and Týr (*Týs ætt*, which begins with the ᛏ = t rune), but this patronage may have been added post hoc. The fact that the *ættir* groupings were kept in the sixteen sign *Fuþark* gives us reasons to believe that it goes back to the origins of the system and that it was regarded as traditional.

Runic writing is also acrophonic, meaning that every rune bears its own name, and its phonetic value is determined by the first phoneme of its name.[2] Every rune follows that acrophonic principle except runes fifteen and twenty-two, z/R (ᛉ) and ŋ (ᛜ), whose phonemes are never the first when spoken; then, the rune bears the name of the last phoneme.

---

2 The phonetic value of each rune was first determined by Sophus Bugge (1883–1907).

The names of runes are always singular. Even when the form of the rune changes, the name stays the same. The first rune's sound, /f/, is associated to the word *fehu, which refers to cattle or wealth (Old Norse fē, Gothic faihu). That term is derived from the Indo-European term *péku, which turned into pecus in Latin (see "pecuniary"). Then came *ūruz "aurochs," *þurisaz "giant," *ansuz "Asa" (ferula), *raidō "ride," etc. That characteristic indicates that Fuþark letters might have been initially some pictographic signs that depicted figuratively the word according to its meaning. Then, the pictograms could have lost their figurative value and become but the sign of the first letter of the word they used to depict figuratively.

Since no runic inscription gave us the names of runes, we got them thanks to fairly recent documents (the oldest ones date back to the 9th century), but their consistency confirms how ancient and stable the names are.[3] Lucien Musset stresses that "there is a substantial consistency among all the nomenclatures, which gives us reason to believe that they share fairly old origins."[4] He adds that "the runes got their names at a time when the Germanic world was still unanimously pagan and relatively united."[5]

The names of runes are mentioned in several manuscripts from the Middle Ages (called *Runica manuscripta*) and four great runic poems.[6] The

---

3   However, some runes' names could have been modified in the Christian period because some of them were considered to be too "pagan." See Maureen Halsall, *The Old English Rune Poem. A Critical Edition*, Toronto University Press, Toronto 1981, p. 15. After the 10th and 11th centuries, runic inscriptions frequently include Christian phrases. Yet, even after Scandinavia was converted to Christianity, some clerical texts still express some distrust and hostility towards runic signs, like *Sólarljóð* ("Song of the sun"), a book on religious edification written at the beginning of the 13th century, which mentions "bloody runes" (*blóðgar rúnir*) and letters "painted with evil signs" (*fáðar feiknstofum*).

4   Lucien Musset, *Introduction à la runologie*, Aubier-Montaigne, Paris 1965, p. 131. Musset's work was in part written based on some of Fernand Mossé's notes. The second edition, which was slightly expanded and improved dates from 1976.

5   Ibid., p. 140. Edgar C. Polomé also believes it is "undeniable that the names transcribed [in the manuscripts] are in all likelihood derived from a common origin, which enabled Wolfgang Krause to make a plausible list of Ancient Germanic names" ("The Names of the Runes," in Alfred Bammesberger, ed., *Old English Runes and their Continental Background*, Carl Winter, Heidelberg 1991, pp. 421–438, quoted here p. 422).

6   On the runic poems, see the important summary of Alessia Bauer, *Runengedichte. Text, Untersuchungen und Kommentare zur gesamten Überlieferung*, Fassbaender,

oldest one is the *Abecedarium Normanicum* or *Nord* (*mannicum*), a text written in Fulda between 801 and 819 at Rabanus Maurus' school (780–856) in a mix of Low German, High German, Anglo-Saxon and Norse. It relates the sixteen runes of the new *Fuþark* and gives their names in alliterative verses: "*Feu forman, / Ur after, / Thuris thritten stabu,*" etc. Then there is the Old English runic poem from the 9th century, the Norwegian runic poem from the end of the 12th century or beginning of the 13th, and the Icelandic runic poem written at most around 1400. The Old English poem was burned in 1731 but its text was saved by a 1731 copy constituted by John Hickes (*Thesaurus I*). That poem gives us the names of the twenty-eight runes of the Anglo-Saxon *Fuþorc*. The Norwegian poem was also burned in a fire in 1728, but we hold copies of it and that gives us the names of the sixteen runes of the new *Fuþark*. The Icelandic Poem also gives us the names of the sixteen rune *Fuþark* under the *kenningar* form, a kind of paraphrasal frequently used in skaldic poetry. The names of runes that were missing from the sixteen sign *Fuþark* have been figured out from a manuscript attributed to Alcuin of Salzburg-Vienna. It dates back to the 9th century and it has Gothic sources.

The last characteristic: since its origins, runic writing can be written from left to right, from right to left, from bottom to top, from top to bottom, in vertical or horizontal lines. It can also be written in boustrophedon mode (meaning that it changes directions at every line like oxen in ploughing). The oldest inscriptions are more often from right to left, while those from the Viking days are mostly from left to right. That detail is important when it comes to finding the origins of runic writing.

Wien 2003. See also René L. M. Derolez, *Runica Manuscripta: The English Tradition*, De Tempel, Brugge 1954.

4

Runic Inscriptions

WE HAVE COME ACROSS 6900 runic inscriptions, and most of them, upwards of 6000, were found in Scandinavia (4000 in Sweden, 1600 in Norway, 850 in Denmark). inscriptions carved in the Old *Fuþark*, numbering no more than 360, are the oldest, and 250 of them were found in Scandinavia, especially in southern Sweden, Jutland, Schleswig, and the Danish Isles (Zealand and Funen). The famous Golden Horns of Gallehus that date back to the 4th century or the first half of the 5th century, discovered in 1639 and 1734 in Denmark near Tondern, are the oldest runic "monument" that we know of. The oldest engraved stone is the one from Möjebro. It seems to date from around 400. New runic inscriptions are discovered regularly and they have been published since 1986 in the Norwegian paper *Nytt om runer. Meldingsblad om runeforskning* (it is a digital publication since 2005).

Older inscriptions are usually very short and hard to decipher. Many of them seem to be some people's names. Only around fifty of them are longer than a couple of words, if they even are words. Out of the 121 old *Fuþark* inscriptions that we can make sense of, seventy-nine are only one line long, forty-four are written from left to right, and thirty-five from right to left. Out of the forty-two that are longer than a line, twenty-four are written in the same direction, and eighteen are written both from left to right and from right to left.

Half of those inscriptions are written on bracteates. Bracteates are thin golden disks with a hole pierced through them so that they can be worn around the neck as pendants. One of their sides bear a decoration, and they were used as jewels, but mostly as amulets. They started being produced around 450. Some of the C type bracteates, the most common type (we know of at least 400 of them), could depict the god Ódhinn, sometimes with his eight-legged horse, Sleipnir, or with his two ravens, Hugin and Munin. Upwards of a hundred bracteates bear a runic inscription.[1]

---

1   Karl Hauck (1916–2007) initiated in 1985 the publication of a colossal seven volume corpus on the entirety of the bracteates found to this day. Three more volumes were added since 2004. Hauck's theories, which associate type C bracteates with the worship of Óðinn and Baldr (Balder) were criticized, especially by Kathryn Starkey, Edgar C. Polomé and Nancy L. Wicker. See Nancy L. Wicker and Henrik Williams, "Bracteates and Runes," in Futhark. *International Journal of Runic Studies*, 3, 2012 [2013], pp. 151–213. See also Morten Axboe, *Brakteatstudier*, Det Kongelige Nordiske Oldskirftselskab, København 2007.

5

The Oldest Inscriptions

AT THE END OF the 19th century, Ludwig F. A. Wimmer was convinced that no runic inscription predated the 4th century. Not so long ago, we thought that no inscription went as far back as the 3rd century. In the 1920s, Maurice Cahen thought that runic writing "could not be dated back further than the 2nd century AD."[1] In 1937, Wolfgang Krause knew of only twelve texts anterior to the end of the 3rd century. Their location indicated that runic writing came into being in the area of current Denmark and then spread to Norway and Sweden, as previously thought. In the 1980s, most people thought roughly the same: that no runic inscriptions were anterior to the end of the 2nd century, but things have subsequently changed.

The dating of the oldest inscriptions is by no means easy. No inscription in old *Fuþark* can be dated historically, which means that their dating relies on archaeology, but also on linguistic data. In many cases, there remains a fairly large degree of uncertainty.[2]

---

1 Maurice Cahen, "Origine et développement de l'écriture runique," in *Mémoires de la Société de linguistique de Paris*, 1923, 1, p. 5.

2 Elmer H. Antonsen goes as far as to think that many objects that date back to the 4th or 5th century could just as well actually go back to the first two centuries AD ("On Runological and Linguistic Evidence for Dating Runic Inscriptions," in Klaus Düwel and Sean Nowak, Hg., *Runeninschriften als Quellen interdisziplinärer Forschung. Abhandlungen des Vierten Internationalen Symposiums über Runen und Runeninschriften in Göttingen vom 4.–9. August 1995*, Walter de Gruyter, Berlin 1998, pp. 150–159; *Runes and Germanic Linguistics*, Mouton de Gruyter, Berlin-New York

Around 1970, the runic inscription that was considered to be the oldest was Øvre Stabu's spearhead, found in a Norwegian tomb around 1890. It bears *raunijaR* as an inscription and we date it back to roughly 150-200 (on the basis of a Roman sword found in the same tomb). Then there was the comb of Vimose, found in Funen (around 150-160) which bears the word *harja* ("warrior"), the two pike tips found in Illerup, Denmark (around 200), and the Værløse fibula (around 200). In the period 250-300, we have the inscription discovered in Mos (Gotland) in 1916, the tip of a sheath from Torsbjerg, the Dahmsdorf spearhead (*ranja*) discovered in 1865 in the Brandeburg tomb, the Kovel spearhead found south of Brest-Litovsk in 1858, etc.

That classic chronology was completely disrupted when in February of 1979, the Meldorf fibula was found in the stockroom of the Schleswig-Holstein regional museum in Schleswig. This bronze 8.5 cm long fibula dates back to the first half, potentially the first quarter, of the 1st century. It bears an inscription that could be *"iþih"* or *"iwih,"* or even *"hiþi"* or *"hiwi,"* depending on the way you read it, but it the meaning is not apparent. Nevertheless, according to Klaus Düwel the word *hiwi* is an etymon for *heiwa-frauja* in Gothic which means "head of the household" (see also *hifrya*, "female head of the household"). But *"iþih"* could also be another name for the god Óðinn.[3]

Does the Meldorf fibula bear a runic inscription? We have several good reasons to believe so. Firstly, there is the fact that the Germanic fibula seems to exclude Latin in favor of runes. However, Bengt Odenstedt claimed in 1983 that it is Latin (*idin*, the dative case for a female noun),[4] which would be surprising since that inscription is most likely read from right to left,

---

2002, p. 167). See also Ulla Lund Hansen, "Die ersten Runen," in Wilhelm Heizmann and Astrid van Nahl (Hg.), *Runica — Germanica — Mediaevalia* [Festschrift Klaus Düwel], Walter de Gruyter, Berlin 2003, pp. 394-398; Wolfgang Beck and Roland Schuhmann, "Die ältesten Runeninschriften im Kontext (sprach)wissenschaftlicher Editionen," in *Futhark. International Journal of Runic Studies*, V, 2014, pp. 7-24.

3 See Mindy MacLeod and Bernard Mees, *Runic Amulets and Magic Objects*, Boydell & Brewer, Woodbridge 2006, p. 23.

4 Bengt Odenstedt, "The Inscription of the Meldorf Fibula," *in Zeitschrift für deutsches Altertum und deutsches Literatur*, 1983, pp. 153-161; "Further Reflections on the Meldorf Inscription," in *Zeitschrift für deutsches Altertum und deutsches Literatur*, 1989, pp. 77-85.

unlike the Latin of that time period (which is read from left to right, as we do today). Klaus Düwel, who remained cautious for a long time, has described it as "proto-runic,"[5] and so does Henrik Williams. Bernard Mees believes that

> the inscription must at least be considered to be proto-runic because it is written on a Germanic fibula, which is an item similar to the first runic artefacts, and because it written in a decorative fashion just like other runic inscriptions from later periods. We can't find Latin inscriptions on such items or with such decorations (the same goes for Greek inscriptions or inscriptions from northern Italy).[6]

If the Meldorf fibula proves to bear runic inscription, its discovery is a breakthrough. It would mean that we now know of a runic inscription 100 or 150 years prior to the one that was considered to be the oldest, and 400 years older than the oldest inscription found in northern Germany.[7] There is also the short inscription (two letters) written on a pottery sherd found in the 1990s in Osterrönfeld, near Rendsford in Schleswig Holstein,[8] and which dates back to 51–100. These two finds, both from German Schleswig "constitute a clear proof that a degree of literacy was already present in

---

5 Klaus Düwel, "The Meldorf Fibula and the Origin of Runic Writing," in Clairborne W. Thompson (ed.), *Proceedings of the First International Symposium on Runes and Runic Inscriptions*, special edition of the Michigan Germanic Studies, printemps 1981, pp. 8–14; Klaus Düwel and Michael Gebühr, "Die Fibel von Meldorf und die Anfänge der Runenschrift," in *Zeitschrift für deutsches Altertum und deutsches Literatur*, 1981, pp. 159–175.

6 Bernard Mees, "Runes in the First Century," in Marie Stoklund, Michael Lerche Nielsen, Bente Holmberg and Gillian Fellows-Jensen (ed.), *Runes and their Secrets. Studies in Runology*, Museum Tusculanum Press, University of Copenhagen, Copenhagen 2006, p. 211.

7 See Bernard Mees, "A New Interpretation of the Meldorf Fibula Inscription," *in Zeitschrift für deutsches Altertum und deutsche Literatur*, 1997, pp. 131–139; Klaus Düwel, "Die Fibel von Meldorf. 25 Jahre Diskussion und kein Ende — zugleich ein kleiner Beitrag zur Interpretationsproblematik und Forschungsgeschichte," in Stefan Burmeister, Heidrun Derks and Jasper von Richthofen (Hg.), *Zweiundvierzig. Festschrift für Michael Gebühr zum 65. Geburtstag*, Marie Leidorf, Rahden/Westf. 2007, pp. 167–174.

8 See Martina Dietz, Edith Marold and Hauke Jöns, "Eine frühkaiserzeitliche Scherbe mit Schriftzeichen aus Osterrönfeld, Kr. Rendsburg-Eckenförde," in *Archäologisches Korrespondenzblatt*, 1996, pp. 179–188.

northern Germany in the first century AD."[9] It is also a proof that, unlike what was previously thought not so long ago, runic writing was already being used in the 1st century.[10]

Of course, it stands to reason that the runes predate the oldest artefacts in which we find them engraved. It is common practice to date the appearance of a script type to a hundred years before its first known manifestation. So, in the case of runes, a 100 or 200 year-long "genesis" period for runic writing seems plausible prior to the inscriptions of Osterrönfeld and Meldorf. Therefore, the runes could have been created before the turn of the millennium.

---

9 Bernard Mees, "Runes in the First Century," art. cit., p. 205.

10 See Klaus Düwel, *Runenkunde*, 4th ed., J. B. Metzler, Stuttgart 2008, pp. 3 and 13.

6

Inscriptions on Wood

THE VAST MAJORITY OF older inscriptions we have found are on spearheads, amulets, bracteates, fibulas, tools or stones. Very few of them (e.g. Illerup, Nydam, Kragehul, Neudingen-Baar) are inscribed in wood. However, many runologists believe that runic inscriptions were originally inscribed in wood. That would explain the angular shape of runes and why they are only made of vertical or diagonal strokes: horizontal strokes would likely hit the wood grain or fibers, and curved shapes would simply be too hard to engrave. Christophe Bord writes that

> the material used to write runic texts is most frequently metal or stone, but we've got reasons to believe that those kinds of material, especially stone, were dedicated to commemorative occasions, and wood was used for other occasions. Since wood rots away, we must relinquish hope of ever finding out the majority of what was written in runes.[1]

That theory makes sense, but it does not make a consensus. Some runic inscriptions inscribed in wooden items found in the swamps of Illerup, Vimose and Nydam (from 200–350) have curved shapes. Nonetheless, those examples are very rare. Linguistics also indicate many etymological links associating the *Fuþark* with wood.

---

1 Christophe Bord, "La "réforme" runique. Matériaux pour une réflexion phonologique," in *Etudes germaniques*, October–December 1997, pp. 527–528.

Beside the word "rune," the most common way to designate runic characters is *stabaR* in Old Nordic, *stafr* in Old Norse meaning "stick," as found in the inscription of Gummarp, from the beginning of the 7th century. The German word *Stab* means "stick, wand, branch." Its combination with *Buche* "beech," turned it into the Old High German word *buohstab* or *buochstap*, into *bokstaf* in Old Saxon, *bocstæf* in Anglo-Saxon meaning "beechstick," then into *bokstaf* in Swedish, and finally *Buchstabe* in German meaning "letter," or literally "piece of beech wood." Supposedly, runes were originally inscribed on wands, tablets, or pieces of beech wood, and that is the reason that the modern word for letters is *Buchstaben*. Since Jakob Grimm, most Germanists tie *boka/bokos*, which means "letter, writing character" in Gothic, to *bōks* or *bōki(o)s*, which means "beech" in common German, and its meaning supposedly changed to "beechstick bearing runes," and then to "book" (in German *Buch*, in English "book"). That explication has been used by some people to claim that there was a cultural connection in ancient times between writing and beech trees.[2] However, this claim is contested, notably by Eduard Sievers, because in most Germanic languages the words "beech" and "book" are gendered differently.

There also is the possibility that the triple alliteration, a characteristic of antiquated German poetry, comes from the three *ættir*. That internal rhyme is called *Stabreim* in German, a substantive that combines *reim*, "rhyme," with *Stab*, "stick, wand."

We should also note that using the verb "to engrave" is the usual way to express the act of "writing," which comes from **wreit-a* in German, **writan* in Old Norse, *rita* in Old Icelandic, *written* in Old Saxon, *wrítan* in Anglo-Saxon, *rizzan* in Old High German, *writs* in Gothic (write shares a common root with *reissen* and *ritzen* which mean "to engrave" in German). All of these words seem to come from an Indo-European root which means "making an incision in something, making a notch in something, engraving." The Greek word *graphein* which means "to write" also originally meant "engrave, trace" (see *grebju* in Latvian, *zerebeji* in Russian, etc.).

---

2   Thomas V. Gamkrelidze and Viaceslav V. Ivanov, *Indo-European and the Indo-Europeans. A Reconstruction and Historical Analysis of a Proto-Language and a Proto-Culture*, vol. 1, Walter de Gruyter, Berlin 1995, p. 533–535.

Venantius Fortunatus who lived in the Merovingian era, was the first writer to unequivocally report on the use of runes by Germanic peoples after the collapse of the Ostrogoth Kingdom of Italy (535–553). After having been appointed the Bishop of Poitiers around the end of the 6th century, he writes to his friend Flavius: "May the barbaric rune be painted on ash wood! / The papyrus' use can also be the polished plank's" (*Barbara fraxineis pingatur rhuna tabellis / Quodque papyrus agit, virgula plana valet*).[3] That account shows that at that time, engraving runes in wood was still a custom.

The original link between runes and wood (or wood engraving) seems to be well established, so it's not a stretch to think — in spite of everything written against that hypothesis, and even if an *argumentum ex silentio* is always risky — that a huge amount of the older runic inscriptions have been lost precisely because they were engraved in this perishable material. Some authors are not afraid to shift the genesis of runic writing further back in time only because all of the first inscriptions were systematically engraved on wood.[4] The hypothesis that some "runic literature" engraved on wood existed but was lost has been defended by Ivar Lindquist[5] and Elias Wessén.[6] Lucien Musset writes that some "texts traced in perishable materials, mostly wood; because their preservation comes only from very exceptional archaeological circumstances, we are unable to assess the real importance of this group of engravings. It is not a stretch to think that they made up the majority of the texts."[7] "What we know," writes Raymond I. Page, "is that what we have now is but a very small fragment of the whole original runic collection."[8]

---

3   Venance Fortunat, Carmina VII, 18, Ad Flavium, 19–20. See Fridericus Leo (Hg.), *Venanti Honori Clementiani Fortunati presbyteri italici opera poetica*, Weidmann, Berlin 1881, p. 173.

4   See Aage Kabell, "Periculum Runicum," in *Norsk Tidsskrift for sprogvidenskab*, 1967, pp. 94–126.

5   Ivar Lindquist, *Religiösa runtexter. II. Sparlösa-stenen. Ett svenskt runmonument från Karl den Stores tid upptäckt 1937. Ett tydningsförslag*, C. W. K. Gleerup, Lund 1940.

6   Elias Wessén, *Runstenen vid Röks kyrka*, Almqvist & Wiksell, Stockholm 1958.

7   *Introduction à la runologie*, op. cit., p. 20.

8   Raymond I. Page, *Runes*, British Museum Publications, London 1987, p. 12.

René Derolez notes that if there were a dozen rune engravers who engraved on average one inscription a month, which seems to be a minimum if we take into account how large the ancient Germanic world was, that would mean that there would have been upwards of 40,000 inscriptions engraved over the span of three centuries, which goes to show how much we are missing, since the forty or fifty runic inscriptions that we have found from the first three centuries are but 1% of that total.[9]

---

9   René L. M. Derolez, "The Runic System and its Cultural Context," in Clairborne W. Thompson (ed.), *Proceedings of the First International Symposium on Runes and Runic Inscriptions*, op. cit., p. 20.

7

The Origin Issue

No single runological issue is more discussed than the origin of runic writing. If we concede that this system of writing is a derived system, then what script does it derive from? Where and when did it become appropriated? Why was that writing created? Who is responsible and how did the runes make their way to Scandinavia? François-Xavier Dillman lays out the problem thusly: "Does runic writing come from an imitation of North Etruscan scripts that were still around in the first century AD near the Alps? Was it a copy of the systems in place in a lot of Latin capitals? Or did it come from the ingenious mind of one or several Germans who became more or less inspired by the Mediterranean alphabetical system, modified it, and added some made-up signs to some existing alphabetical signs, or even repurposed a potential stock of symbolic strokes from prehistory?"[1] Those are the questions left unanswered.

Raymond I. Page noticed that "for every runic inscription, there are as many interpretations as runologists studying it."[2] Indeed, many inscriptions are hard to decipher, and the results are seldom unanimously agreed upon

---

1 François-Xavier Dillmann, "Tripartition fonctionnelle et écriture runique en Scandinavie à l'époque païenne," in Jacques Bonnet (ed.), *Georges Dumézil*, op. cit., p. 249. See also Ottar Grønvik, *Über die Bildung des älteren und des jüngeren Runenalphabets*, Peter Lang, Frankfurt/M. 2001; Wilhelm Heizmann, "Zur Entstehung der Runenschrift," in John Ole Askedal and al. (Hg.), *Zentrale Probleme bei der Erforschung der älteren Runen*, op. cit., pp. 9–32.

2 *Mediaeval Scandinavia*, 1970, p. 202.

(especially since few runologists can study inscriptions "in person" since they are unable to examine them *in situ*). In that matter, Klaus Düwel adds that "everything is thinkable, a lot of things are in the realm of possibility, a few are plausible, nothing is certain."[3] The same goes for their origins. "There is nothing we know for sure about the origins of the runes," writes Wolfgang Krause.[4] In such circumstances, it is obvious that "the only wise approach ... is to stick as much as possible to the observable facts."[5] However, when those "observable facts" are not enough to answer the questions we keep coming across, when we have to rely on conjectures, it is not only warranted but also necessary to form hypotheses to figure out which of them is the best at explaining that which we do not know. Inductive logic can be very useful in that matter by helping in sorting out the plausible and likely. Nonetheless, we must not give in to political pressure that sometimes obfuscates debates — like (but not limited to) what happened in 1920s and 1930s Germany[6] — as well as completely wild suppositions that keep the minds of amateur "runologists" heated.[7]

The idea that the *Fuþark* derives from another script, which contradicts the autochthonous theory that was still held in 1929 by the Germanist Gustav

---

3   *Runenkunde*, op. cit., p. VI.

4   Wolfgang Krause, Runen, Walter de Gruyter, Berlin 1970. That quote is from the French edition of the book: *Les runes*, Le Porte-Glaive, Paris 1995, p. 51.

5   Lucien Musset, op. cit., p. 36.

6   On runology in the Third Reich, one should refer to the excellent work of Ulrich Hunger, *Die Runenkunde im Dritten Reich*, Peter Lang, Frankfurt/M. 1984.

7   We shall mention Guido (von) List's "ariosophic" deliriums only for the record (*Das Geheimnis der Runen*, Zillman, Groß-Lichterfelde 1908; *Die Bilderschrift der Ario-Germanen*, G. von List Gesellschaft, 1910), who imagined an original runic alphabet of eighteen "armanist" runes (the *Armanen-Runen*), some from the young *Fuþark*, the others ("Eh" and "Gibor") are the fruits of his imagination. Guido (von) List's theories (1848–1919) were picked up after him by Friedrich Bernhard Marby (1882–1966) and Rudolf Arnold Spieth. In that same category of crazy people, there are authors like Siegfried Adolf Kummer (*Heilige Runenmacht*, Uranus, Hemburg 1932), Rudolf Gorsleben (*Hoch-Zeit der Menschen*, Koehler u. Amelang, Leipzig 1930), Philipp Strauff, Karl Spiesberger (*Runenmagie*, Schikowski, Berlin 1955), Ulrich Jürgen Heinz, Kenneth Meadows, David V. Barrett, Igor Warneck, Ralph Tegtmeier, Ralph Blum, Reinhard Florek and many other practitioners of "runic gymnastics," "runic yoga," "runic meditation," "runic astrology," "runic rituals," "runic oracles," "Runelore" of the New Age kind etc.

Neckel,[8] relies on the proposition that runic writing appeared immediately under an "alphabetical" form when every other writing seems to have first gone through pictographic, ideographic or syllabographic stages. The great resemblance between runes and letters from Mediterranean scripts which are much older than runic writing (and also derive from the Phoenician alphabet) was noted since the beginnings of runology. So naturally there are three main theories: they either explain runic writing by an appropriation of the Latin script, the Greek script, or of scripts from northern Italy ("North Etruscan").

---

8   Gustav Neckel, "Zur Frage nach dem Ursprung der Runen," in *Studier tillägnade Axel Kock*, Gleerup, Lund 1929, pp. 371–375.

8

The Latin Theory

THE THEORY THAT RUNIC writing is derived from Latin was first held by Ludwig F. A. Wimmer in 1874, a man considered to be the father of modern runology.[1] According to him, runic writing was created between the end of the 2nd century and the beginning of the 3rd century by a German who lived next to the Roman *limes* in southern Germany and was inspired by the city of Rome in its Imperial period. The issue then is that the older runic inscriptions of that time (the Kowel spearhead, the Pietroassa bracelet, etc.) were found in eastern Europe and written in the Gothic language. "How could it be that runes show up so late in western Europe, which is supposed to be their birthplace?" asks Maurice Cahen.[2]

Holger Pedersen goes over the Latin theory in 1923,[3] but he thinks that the Celts were probably an intermediary between the Romans and the Germanic people, which is why he emphasizes the similarities between runic writing and Ogham: their peculiar orders compared to Mediterranean

---

1 Ludwig F. A. Wimmer, "Die ældste nordiske runeindskrifter," in *Aarbøger for nordisk oldkyndighed og historie*, 1867; *Runeskriftens oprindelse og udvikling i Norden*, V. Prior, København 1874 (trad. all.: *Die Runenschrift*, Weidmann, Berlin 1887); "Runeskriftens oprindelse og udvikling i Norden," in *Aarbøger for nordisk oldkyndighed og historie*, 1894, pp. 1–170; *Les monuments runiques de l'Allemagne*, Thiele, Copenhagen 1895.

2 "Origine et développement de l'écriture runique," art. cit., p. 6.

3 Holger Pedersen, "Runernes oprindelse," in *Aarbøger for nordisk oldyndighed og historie*, 1923; "L'origine des runes," in *Mémoires de la Société royale des antiquaires du Nord*, 1920–1924, pp. 88–136.

alphabets, the groupings of their letters, the fact that letters bear acrophonic names, the fact that both the *Fuþark* and Ogham have a sign for the ŋ letter.[4] He therefore thinks that both the Germanic and Irish peoples created their alphabets in a Celtic environment influenced by Latin. That borrowing is supposed to have taken place in the beginning of the 1st century in the Rhine region. That theory of an alphabet which served as a common model for *Fuþark* and Ogham was approved by Fernand Mossé. Twenty years later, Fritz Askeberg believes that based on new runic inscriptions from

---

4   The Ogham was used in the first centuries after Christ to write Old Irish and Brittonic languages. The phonemes are divided into four five-sign groups, "*aicmí*" (plural) or *aicme* (singular). Three of those groups represent consonants, and the fourth one represents the vowels. A fifth group which comprises five diphtongs (*forfeda*) was added later on. See Christian J. Guyonvarc'h, "Die irische Ogam-Schrift," in *Studium Generale*, 1967, 7, pp. 448–456. The "letters" (*feda*) are represented with notches or dashes along a straight line which usually corresponds to the edge of a stone. Every sign bears the name of a tree or a plant, which explains why this "alphabet" is often called bethe-luis-nin "birch-elm-ash" based on its three first letters. We know their names thanks to Irish grammar manuscripts called *Auraicept na n-Eces* ("the Poet's fundamental book"), which date from the 14th century (see George Calder, ed., *Book of Ballymote*, John Grant, Edinburgh 1917, pp. 272–276). Approximately 350 Ogham inscriptions were found, most of them in southern Ireland or in Wales. They are generally very short and are about incantations or magic. The oldest ones seem to date from the 4th century—but James Carney relies on phonological arguments to claim that they go back to the 1st century (*The Invention of the Ogam Cipher* "Eriu," Royal Irish Academy, Dublin 1975, p. 57. See also Joseph Vendryès, "L'écriture ogamique et ses origins," in Etudes celtiques, 1931, 4, pp. 110–113). Irish tradition attributes the discovery of the Ogham to the god Ogmius/Ogmios, brother of the Dagda, the Celtic Jupiter. Just like Óðinn in the Germanic religion, Ogmios is a "binding" god, a representative of the night sky who is linked to magic. Two stones from the medieval period were found in the Isle of Man (Maughold Stone and Kirk Michael Stone). They bore both Ogham characters and runes. The theory that runic writing and the Ogham share a common origin has been defended by the Norwegian Carl S. Mastrander (1928). Alan Griffiths believes that the *Fuþark* and the Ogham are both derived from a common Greek alphabet. See Alan Griffiths, "The *Fuþark* (and Ogam): Order as a Key to Origin," in *Indogermanische Forschungen*, 1999, pp. 164–210; "Rune-names: The Irish Connexion," in Marie Stoklund, Michael Lerche Nielsen, Bente Holmberg and Gillian Fellows-Jensen (ed.), *Runes and their Secrets*, op. cit., pp. 83–116. On the comparaison of the Ogham and the runes, see also Helmut Birkhan, "Keltisches in germanischen Runennamen?," in Alfred Bammesberger and Gaby Waxenberger (Hg.), *Reallexikon der Germanischen Altertumskunde*, vol. 51, Walter de Gruyter, Berlin 2006. The origin of the Ogham, its potentials connections with runic writing, as well as whether the alphabetical Ogham is but a secondary use of the Ogham are the source of various theories that we won't examine here.

east Germany, Poland and Russia it's very unlikely that runic writing came from a territory occupied by the Romans and that it must have come from the Goths living near the Vistula in the second century and inspired by the Latin alphabet.[5]

Thanks to Askeberg's work, Erik Moltke developed in 1951 the theory that runic writing was created by Danish merchants from Latin.[6] He argues that runic writing couldn't have come "from any Etruscan territory or any territory under Etruscan influence," citing how Denmark (especially Scania) was very likely to be the birthplace of runic writing, and also the undeniable fact that lasting relations existed between Rome and Scandinavia. The runes would supposedly come from the Roman uppercase writing from the imperial period and would supposedly have been created at a time when trade with the Romans was increasing.[7] They would supposedly be more or less contemporary of the existence of Jesus, with a margin of error of fifty years later and 100 years before. Moltke's theory, which suggests a Rhineland intermediary, assumes that the invention of runic writing served purely utilitarian purposes, but then why didn't the Danish merchants simply use Latin?[8] And why don't the oldest runic inscriptions have any "commercial" or utilitarian characteristics?

---

5   Fritz Askeberg, *Norden och kontinenten i gammal tid. Studier i forngermansk kulturhistoria*, Almqvist & Wiksell, Uppsala 1944.

6   Erik Moltke, "Er runeskriften opstaæt in Danmark?," in Nationalmuseets arbejdsmark, 1951, pp. 47–58; *Runerne i Danmark og deres oprindelse*, Forum, København 1976; "The Origines of the Runes," in Clairborne W. Thompson (ed.), *Proceedings of the First International Symposium on Runes and Runic Inscriptions*, op. cit., pp. 3–18; *Runes and their Origin. Denmark und Elsewhere*, National Museum of Denmark, Copenhagen 1985. That last publication was published the day after its author's death.

7   On the influence the Greco-Roman civilization had in Denmark, see Lisbeth M. Imer, "Latin og græsk i romersk jernalder. Fremmed indflydelse på Nordens tidligste runeskrift," in *Aarbøger for nordisk oldkyndighed og historie*, 2004 [2007], pp. 63–105.

8   The Germanic people definitely encountered Latin writing very early on. To this day, at least forty-nine inscriptions in Latin that go back to the first 160 years after Christ, most of them being on bronze objects, have been found in Scandinavia and especially in Denmark. See Lisbeth M. Imer, "Runes and Romans in the North," in *Futhark. International Journal of Runic Studies*, 1, 2010, pp. 41–64. In his *Annals* (II, 63, 1), Tacitus evokes a letter that Maroboduus sent to Tiberius. In another passage (II, 88, 1), he says that in the time of Arminius, a leader of the Chatti called upon the Roman Senate in writing. He does not mention the writing that was used in those missives, but one can reasonably assume that they were written in Latin. Ammianus Marcellinus

In spite of being violently criticized by Elmer H. Antonsen,[9] the Latin theory remains the one currently approved by most runologists. Bengt Odenstedt recently supported it and he too believes that the Goths created runic writing,[10] as does Elmar Seebold who, like Pedersen, believes in a Celtic intermediary,[11] and Henrik Williams who believes that the runes were derived from uppercase Latin writing.[12] Similarly, Gad Rausing[13] and Arend Quak believe it was rather derived from cursive Latin, and like Wilhelm Heizmann and Marie Stoklund, the latter believing that the birthplace of runic writing is Zeeland.[14] Klaus Düwel also thinks, with reserve, that it was borrowed from the Latin language at the very beginning of the 1st century.

---

mentions a message written by a Germanic leader to his people, but there again in a Roman context (XXIX, 4, 7). Those indications show that the Germanic people weren't illiterate, and that some of them knew the Latin language. Hence the question: why didn't they pick up Latin writing? Svante Fischer sees in the appearance of runic writing a reaction against "Roman imperialism," which was born out of a "desire to imitate the Roman imperialist ideology." (*Roman Imperialism and Runic Literacy. The Westernization of Northern Europe*, 150–800 AD, Department of Archaeology and Ancient History, Uppsala University, Uppsala 2005, p. 45).

9   *Runes and Germanic Linguistics*, op. cit., pp. 93–99.
10 Bengt Odenstedt, *On the Origin and Early History of the Runic Script. Typology and Graphic Variation in the Older Futhark*, Gustav Adolf Akademien, Uppsala 1990.
11 Elmar Seebold, "Die Herkunft der Runenschrift," in John Ole Askedal, Harald Bjorvand and Eyvind Fjeld Halvorsen (Hg.), *Festskrift til Ottar Grønvik på 75-årsdagen den 21. Oktober 1991*, Universitetsforlaget, Oslo 1991, pp. 16–32.
12 Henrik Williams, "The Origin of the Runes," in Tineke Looijenga et Arend Quak (ed.), *Frisian Runes and Neighbouring Traditions. Proceedings of the First International Symposium on Frisian Runes at the Fries Museum, Leeuwarden 26-29 January 1994*, Rodopi, Amsterdam 1996, pp. 211–218; "Reasons for Runes," in Stephen D. Houston (ed.), *The First Writing. Script Invention as History and Process*, Cambridge University Press, Cambridge 2004, pp. 262–273.
13 Gad Rausing, "On the Origin of the Runes," in *Fornvännen*, 1992, pp. 200–205; Arend Quak, "Noch einmal die Lateinthese," in Tineke Looijenga and Arend Quak (ed.), *Frisian Runes and Neighbouring Traditions*, op. cit., pp. 171–179.
14 Wilhelm Heizmann, "Zur Entstehung der Runenschrift," art. cit.; Marie Stoklund, "Die erste Runen — Die Schriftsprache der Germanen," in Lars Jørgensen, Birger Storgaard and Lone Gebauer Thomsen (Hg.), Sieg und Triumpf. Der Norden im Schatten des Römischen Reiches, Nationalmuseet, Kopenhagen 2003, pp. 172–179; "Chronology and Typology of the Danish Runic Inscriptions," in Marie Stoklund, Michael Lerche Nielsen, Gillian Fellows-Jensen and Bente Holmberg (ed.), Runes and their Secrets. Studies in Runology, Museum Tusculanum Press, Copenhagen 2006, pp. 355–383.

He is backed by François-Xavier Dillman who believes that "the shape of most runic signs was clearly inspired by the characters of Latin writing."[15]

The Latin theory is obviously based on the reality of Roman presence and influence in western Europe. The general idea is that the numerous cultural and commercial connections between the Romans and the Germanic people could only lead the latter to develop some vernacular writing, and that would also explain the close similarity of some runes with Latin letters. The similarities are quite obvious between Latin and the r, f, þ, i, t, v, l and b letters of runic writing. There are also shape- and sound-based similarities for five more runes: a, c (or k), d, o and s, but for p, m and x the shape similarities do not match the phonetic similarities. Lastly, seven runes have no equivalent whatsoever in the Latin alphabet: g (ᚷ), n (ᚾ), j (ᛃ), ï (ᛇ), p (ᛈ), z/R (ᛉ), ŋ (ᛜ) and d (ᛞ). Moltke thinks the differences between the Fuþark and the Latin alphabet are due to the borrowing being "indirect," which does not mean much. John S. Robertson has a somewhat complex theory inspired by Jerzy Kurlowicz's "the 4th law of analogical change" to explain those differences.[16] The people behind the Latin borrowing theory explain the -io or -ijo ending of some names in runic inscriptions by an influence of the -ius Latin endings.

---

15 François-Xavier Dillmann, "L'écriture runique," in Anne-Marie Christin (ed.), *Histoire de l'écriture, de l'idéogramme au multimédia* [2001], 2nd ed., Flammarion, Paris 2012, p. 279. The same expression can be found in "La connaissance des runes dans l'Islande ancienne," communication prononcée à l'Académie des Inscriptions et Belles-lettres le 6 février 2009 (*Comptes rendus de l'Académie des Inscriptions et Belles-lettres. Séances de l'année 2009, janvier-mars*, Paris 2009 [paru en décembre 2010], pp. 241–276). See also, from the same author, "Les runes, écriture des Vikings," in *Les Dossiers d'archéologie*, April 1992, pp. 20–29. On the Latin theory, See also Terje Spurkland, "The Older 'Futhark' and Roman Script Literacy," in *Futhark. International Journal of Runic Studies*, 1, 2010, pp. 65–84.

16 John S. Robertson, "How the Germanic Futhark Came from the Roman Alphabet," in *Futhark. International Journal of Runic Studies*, 2, 2001 [2012], pp. 7–25. The fourth out of six laws of analogical change stated in 1949 by Jerzy Kurylowicz is the following: "When a form is subjected to differentiation after having gone through a morphological transformation, the new form corresponds to the primary function (founding function), and its old form is reserved for the secondary function (founded function)." See Jerzy Kurylowicz, "La nature des procès dits 'analogiques'," in *Acta linguistica*, 1966, pp. 121–138.

However, this theory has two issues: firstly, in most of its versions, the theory does not give enough time for the runes to realistically migrate or spread to northern Europe, meaning that the timespan between the initial borrowing and the appearance of the first runic inscriptions in Scandinavia is too short to be plausible. Secondly, classical Latin was never written from right to left nor in boustrophedon[17] at that time, whereas it is common practice in runic writing, which jeopardizes the credibility of the borrowing.

---

[17] See Ernst Meyer, *Einführung in die lateinische Epigraphik*, Wissenschaftliche Buchgesellschaft, Darmstadt 1973, p. 37. Runic inscriptions on stone monuments (*bautarsteinar*) can sometimes be vertical, whereas in Roman epigraphy, letters are always laid out horizontally.

9

The Greek Theory

AS EARLY AS IN 1899, the Norwegian Sophus Bugge tried to remedy the imperfections of theories by arguing that runic writing has a dual ancestry: some runes come from Latin while others — n, þ, o, e, g, w — come from the Greek alphabet. Like other runologists, he thought that the Goths were the first to use runic writing, and that they spread it to other Germanic peoples. Moreover, he believed in an Armenian intermediary for the Greek language. This peculiar theory was furthered in 1904 by Otto von Friesen who thought that sixteen runes came from the Greek alphabet, three from Greco-Latin cursive, and four from (ᚠ, ᚾ, ᚱ, ᚺ) the Latin alphabet.[1] Otto von Friesen believes like Bugge (with whom he shares conclusions) that the Fuþark was created in the Pontus region (Black Sea) and he gives the credit to Gothic mercenaries that served in Roman legions. The borrowing is supposed to have taken place in the first half of the 2nd century. The theory which acquired the support of the Swedish archaeologist Bernhard Salin[2] (and whose explanation of the similarities between the ᛟ rune and omega can be counted as an asset) became popular after it was published in the 1919 edition of the *Encyclopaedia Britannica*.

---

[1] Otto von Friesen, "Om runskriftens härkomst," in *Språkvetenskapliga sällskapets i Uppsala förhandlingar*, 1904, pp. 1–55; "Runskriftens härkomst," in *Nordisk Tidsskrift för filologi*, 1913, p. 161–180; *Röstenen i Bohuslän och runorna i Norden*, Almqvist & Wiksell, Uppsala 1924.

[2] Bernhard Salin and Johanna Mestorf, *Die altgermanische Thierornamentik*, K. L. Beckmann, Stockholm 1904.

But the Greek theory also faces obstacles formulated as early as 1923 by the Dane Holger Pedersen, which were summed up by Lucien Musset in the words:

> Firstly, how can we believe that people sought a cursive and hand-written writing to make an epigraphic writing when Latin or Greek provided that so well with their upper-case letters? Moreover, there's nothing to account for the supposed influence Greek civilization had on Goths before the conversion of the Goths in Moesia to Christianism in the 4th century [...] Lastly, the timespan related to the spreading of runes now seem much too short: the Goths didn't make it to the shores of the Black Sea until 238, at best until the beginning the 3rd century.[3]

It's indeed not quite plausible that the creators of runic writing were inspired by Greek cursive writing rather than capital letters that were used in that period as evidenced by remaining monuments.[4] Besides, Greek from that period also wasn't written from right to left nor in boustrophedon. Lastly, the Greek alphabet doesn't have a letter that matches þ (th) which is found in runic writing. That explains why Otto von Friesen had to also turn to Latin for his theory.

But the issue is mainly with the Goths reference. The Goths settled along a trade route from the Baltic Sea to the Black Sea in the 2nd century, following the flow of the Vistula and the Dnieper. In the beginning of the 3rd century, they created a Germanic cultural center on the northern and northwestern shores of the Black Sea. In Otto von Friesen's time, people thought that the oldest runic inscriptions were Gothic. The Kowel spearhead has *tilarīd* inscribed on it, and that seems to be written in Gothic. The great golden necklace found in 1837 in Pietroassa, Romania, has *gutaniowihailag* inscribed on it, and *gutani* could be the Goths' ethnic name (they were called *Gutones* in Latin). The spearhead of Dahmsdorf that was found in a tomb in Brandeburg could also be Gothic as it has *ranja* inscribed in it. But the Goths only came in contact with the Romans in 214, and we now know that the first runic inscriptions were written well before their settlement in

---

3   *Introduction à la runologie*, p. 45.

4   Caesar says about the Helvetians that knew and used "Greek letters" (*graecis litteris*), and that some tablets inscribed with a "Greek" writing were found in their camp (*De bello gallico*, I, 29, 1; VI, 14, 3).

the Black Sea region. Therefore, it is not possible to consider them as the inventors of runes for chronological reasons. Some people even contest the claim that the Goths knew about runic writing.[5]

The Greek theory has been recently perpetuated by Martin Giertz in his response to Gad Rausing,[6] and by Aage Kabell, Elmer H. Antonsen and Richard L. Morris, but their formulations are very different and we will review them later on in this book.

---

[5] See James W. Marchand, "Les Gots ont-ils vraiment connu l'écriture runique?," in *Mélanges Fernand Mossé*, pp. 277–291. On the inscriptions that we just mentioned, the author assures us that "If one examines them up close, one cannot affirm with certainty that they are Gothic" (p. 278). Regarding the inscription of Pietroassa, *gutaniowihailag*, that was interpreted as *Gutani ō(ð)al wī(þ)hailag* "hereditary property of the Goths, established and inviolable," he writes that "it isn't even certain that gutanio refers to the name of the Goths." Moreover, it isn't confirmed that the Goths used the word *hailag(s)* "sacred" They rather used the word weihs which means the same thing. Marchand also contests the widespread idea that the bishop Ulfilas used some runic signs in the Gothic alphabet he invented to translate the Bible in the 4th century. The question whether the first inscriptions comprised a "Gothic" linguistic element is actually controversial since the days of Sophus Bugge. Rasmus Rask, who was in the 19th century one of the founders of comparative philology held an element he called gotisk in that regard. He refused to assimilate it to the *germanisk* ("Germanic") or the *tysk* ("german"), like Jakob Grimm did. Peter Andreas Munch (1847) also believed there was some "Gothic" in the language used for the inscription of Golden Horns of Gallehus. In 1929 Carl J. S. Marstrander made a list of fourteen inscriptions that were according to him written in Gothic by the Heruli. Wolfgang Krause cut it down to four in 1966. Lena Peterson and then Klaus Düwel became even more skeptical ("A Critical Survey of the Alleged East Germanic Runic Inscriptions in Scandinavia," in Klaus Düwel, Hg., *Runeninschriften als Quellen interdisziplinärer Forschung*, op. cit., pp. 556–575). See also Hans Frede Nielsen, "Gothic Runic Inscriptions in Scandinavia?," in *Futhark. International Journal of Runic Studies*, 2, 2011 [2012], pp. 51–61.

[6] Martin Giertz, "Replik till Gad Rausings debattinläg i *Fornvännen* 87, 'On the Origin of the Runes'" in *Fornvännen*, 1993, pp. 27–28.

10

The North Italic Theory

DATED TO THE 5th century BC, the alphabets of northern Italy (which used to be called "north-Etruscan") were used by the Cisalpine Gauls, the Veneti people, the Illyrians, the Celto-Ligures, the Rhaetians and the Lepontii. The alphabets prevailed against proper Etruscan writing for a time, which vanished in the middle of the 1st century BC. We know of four major types: The Lugano type (region of the Lake Maggiore and the Lake Lugano) the Bolzano/Bozen (South Tyrol) type, the Sondrio (upper Adda region) type, those three types forming the "sub-alpine group," and then there is the Veneti alphabets group and its "Illyrian" dialect which are used from the region of Este and Padua to the border of Carinthia. All those scripts seem to be derived from a western Greek alphabet that is somewhat close to the one which was the source of the Etruscan alphabet in Tuscany. They started to lose ground to Latin as early as the 2nd century BC. The last one to disappear were the Veneti types, and they vanished in the beginning of the 1st century.

As early as 1856, the German Karl Weinhold alluded to the possibility of a *Fuþark* derivation from a north-Etruscan alphabet.[1] In 1873, Sophus Bogge wondered if the Germanic people had known and adopted that alphabet through the intermediary of a Celtic tribe from the Alps. But it is

---

1   Karl Weinhold, *Altnordisches Leben*, Weidmann, Berlin 1856.

the publication of north Italic material at the end of the 19th century[2] that really blew wind into the sails of the third theory (called the "Etruscan," "north-Etruscan" or "north Italic" theory) and made it able to compete with the Greek and Latin theories. That new theory was laid out in 1928 by the Norwegian Carl J. S. Marstrander, and then expanded the following year by the Finn Magnus Hammarström.

After having discarded the Latin theory because the phonemes of four runes do not exist in Latin, and after having put the Greek theory to one side because it did not appeal to him, Carl J. S. Marstrander brought up the theory that runic writing was derived from the Rhaetian alphabets of Magre, Sondrio and Bolzano, and the Lepontii alphabet of Lugano. He attributes it to the Marcomanni of Bohemia and Moravia, who supposedly spread the runes to the Goths and the Germanic peoples of northern Europe in the second half of the 1st century.[3] The Marcomanni ("the walkers, or frontiersmen") whose most famous king is Maroboduus, are Suebi who first settled in Thuringia and Saxony. In Caesar's time, they are to be found near the Helvetians on the upper stream of the Rhine. They then settled in the alpine regions to found a stable state, an area with Etruscans and Ligures, and then Illyrians and Venetis, all of whom had cultures that were absorbed by Celtic populations in the 4th century BC. Marstrander used this to argue, like Holger Pedersen before him, that the beginnings of runic writing had a direct impact on Ogham writing.

To back up his views, Marstrander used a runic inscription on a bone fragment found in 1924 in Maria Saal in Carinthia that was thought to date to the roughly the year 100, which made it the oldest known inscription. Unfortunately, it turned out to be a fake. He also uses the Negau B helmet, which seems more susceptible to prove his theory. That helmet, that was found in Zenjak Negova (Negau), comes from a Celtic sanctuary on the border of Noricum and Pannonia. It is usually dated to 1st or 2nd century, but it may be older, possibly belonging to an auxiliary recruited by the Roman

---

2   Carl Pauli, *Die Inschriften nord-etruskischen Alphabets*, Barth, Leipzig 1885.

3   Carl J. S. Marstrander, "Om runene og runenavnenes oprindelse," in *Norsk Tidsskrift for sprogvidenskap*, 1928, pp. 5–179 (with a summary in French, pp. 180–188). Based on the spearhead of Øvre Stabu, Haakon Shetelig (Préhistoire de la Norvège, H. Aschehoug, Oslo 1926) he also believed it was the Marcomanni. It was also the opinion of Karl Simon (1928).

army to fight the Illyrian uprising in the years 6–9. It bears on its external side a fourteen-character-long inscription in north Etruscan written from right to left: *hariXastiteiva*, which seems to be a consecration "to the god Harigasti(z)." Harigast or Herigast could be another way to call Óðinn as God of war, whereas Teiwaz (*tiwaz) is the dative case of Týr's name (later Ziu). So we have an archaic Germanic inscription, admitted as such in 1925, but which was drawn with Etruscan letters. Is it enough to make it the "missing link" between the sub-alpine alphabets and the first Germanic runes? Marstrander purported it to be the proof that an ancient Germanic person was familiar enough with "north Etruscan" writing to have used it to transcribe his own language. Robert Nedoma and Thomas L. Markey then picked up where he left off.[4]

Magnus Hammarström picked up in 1929 the thesis put forward by Marstrander but, by relying on the fact that north Italic alphabets kept some archaic traits from the old Greek alphabet (like writing from right to left, or the absence of the double consonant, which is also the case for runic writing), he put the creation of the *Fuþark* back to between 150 BC and the beginning of the 1st century.[5] According to him, the origin of runic writing is to be found in a sub-alpine alphabet already heavily influenced by Latin, which supposedly eventually spread to northern Europe through the Marcomanni or Celtic populations from the Alps.

The discovery of new North-Etruscan inscriptions, like the vase of Castaneda (Grisons canton, Switzerland) that dates back to the 5th century BC and bears an inscription in the Sondrio alphabet, as well as several inscriptions in Nordic writing found on slopes of the Magdalenensberg, in Carinthia, gave more backing to the idea of an affiliation between runic writing and north Italic alphabets.

That allowed the north Italic theory to find success. In the 1930s and 1940s, Helmut Arntz carries it on but instead of involving the Marcomanni,

---

4 Robert Nedoma, *Die Inschrift auf dem Helm B von Negau. Möglichkeiten und Grenzen der Deutung norditalischer epigraphischer Denkmäler*, Fassbaender, Wien 1995; Thomas L. Markey, "A Tale of the Two Helmets: Negau A and B," in *The Journal of Indo-European Studies*, 2001, pp. 69–172.

5 Magnus Hammarström, "Om runskriftens härkomst," in *Studier i nordisk filologi*, 1929, pp. 1–67.

he involved the Cimbri who supposedly spread runic writing to central Germany after their defeat at the battle of Vercellæ in 101 BC. That is, if the creators were not in actually some Germanic tribes in the northwestern Alps that settled in northern Italy in the 4th century BC (the Alpengermanen as Pytheas and Livy called them), and of whom we know little except that their members served in the Celtic and then Roman militaries as mercenaries.[6]

In 1939, Franz Altheim and Elisabeth Trautmann picked up this theory but altered it.[7] They too thought that the Cimbri spread the runes to central Germany and then to their original territory, but they stressed that the borrowing could also have taken place in northern Noricum or in the Brenner region when the Cimbri retreated to south Germany after being beaten in the battle of Noreja in 113 BC, or also in north Italy, in the Transpadane region where they were located in 102-101 BC. Altheim and Trautmann had more confidence in the second hypothesis, which enabled them to suppose that the Cimbri also borrowed from the Rupestrian engravings of the Val Camonica. So, runic writing would supposedly originate from a fusion of a north Italic alphabet and some magical/religious symbols and pictograms borrowed from those rupestrian engravings.

After WWII, the north Italy theory was picked up by Karl Schneider, Otto Haas[8] and Ralph W. V. Elliot.[9] Lucien Musset was siding with it and underlined that

> from a typological standpoint, the general resemblance between North Etruscan alphabet and the *Fuþark* is striking. There are signs in the Lugano

---

6   Helmut Arntz, *Handbuch der Runenkunde*, Max Niemeyer, Halle/Saale 1935 (2nd ed. 1944). It should be noted that at the time the publication faced some backlash in official circles. See the violent critique of Edmund Weber, "Ein Handbuch der Runenkunde," in *Germanien*, September 1937, pp. 257-260. Helmut Arntz was also virulently criticized by the prehistorian Hans Reinerth. On the "Germanic people of the Alps" see Hans Schmeja, *Der Mythos von den Alpengermanen*, Gerold, Wien 1968; Klaus Düwel, "Alpengermanen," in Heinrich Beck et al. (Hg.), *Reallexikon der Germanischen Altertumskunde*, vol. 1, Walter de Gruyter, Berlin 1973, pp. 190-191.

7   Franz Altheim and Elisabeth Trautmann, *Vom Ursprung der Runen*, Deutsches Ahnenerbe, Frankfurt/M. 1939.

8   Otto Haas, "Die Herkunft der Runenschrift," in *Lingua Posaniensis*, 1955, pp. 41-58; "Die Herkunft der Runenschrift," in *Orbis*, 1965, pp. 216-236.

9   Ralph W. V. Elliott, *Runes. An Introduction* [1959], Manchester University Press, Manchester 1971, p. 6.

and Rhaetian alphabets, especially the Sondrio and Bolzano ones, whose analogy with runes are too great to be fortuitous.

However, he added that this does not make the North Etruscan hypothesis a "proven truth," but that it was the "most satisfying one in existence to explain the facts currently known."[10] It was also backed by Thomas L. Markey[11], Bernard Mees[12] or Helmut Rix,[13] and the latter used the inscriptions of the Val Camonica to justify his position. The north Italy theory has also received the back of several Italian researchers like Vittore Pisani or Aldo Luigi Prosdocimi.[14]

The north Italy theory is convincing mainly because it accounts for the "archaic" character of the *Fuþark* much better than the Greek and Latin theories do. Indeed, the north Etruscan writings kept some archaic traits (for instance that it is written from right to left or in boustrophedon) at a time when they were completely removed from the Greek and Latin alphabets. That theory also fits nicely with what we currently know about runic writing, meaning that it was created sooner than we thought. Since north Italic languages have been replaced by Latin at the latest in the middle of the 1st century BC, it means that if they are responsible for the birth of runic writing, then runic writing must have been appeared before that time. That is why Ralph W. V. Elliot pushed the creation of runic writing back to 250–150 BC.[15]

---

10 *Introduction à la runologie*, op. cit., pp. 47 and 49.

11 Thomas L. Markey, "Studies in Runic Origins," in *American Journal of Germanic Linguistic and Literatures*, 1998, pp. 153–200, and 1999, pp. 131–203.

12 Bernard Mees, "The North Etruscan Thesis of the Origin of the Runes," in *Arkiv för nordisk filologi*, 2000, pp. 33–82.

13 Helmut Rix, "Thesen zum Ursprung der Runenschrift," in Luciana Aigner-Foresti (ed.), *Etrusker nördlich von Etrurien. Etruskische Präsenz in Norditalien und nördlich der Alpen sowie ihre Einflüsse auf die einheimischen Kulturen. Akten des Symposions von Wien-Neuwaldegg, 2.–5. Oktober 1989*, Verlag der Österreichischen Akademie der Wissenschaften, Wien 1992, pp. 411–441.

14 Vittore Pisani, "Italische Alphabete und germanische Runen," in *Zeitschrift für vergleichende Sprachforschung*, 1966, pp. 199–211; Aldo Luigi Prosdocimi, "L'origine delle rune come trasmissione di alphabeti," in *Studi linguistici e filologici per Carlo Alberto Mastrelli*, Pisa 1985, pp. 387–399; "Sulla formazione dell'alfabeto runico. Promessa di novità documentali forse decisive," in *Archivio per Alto Adige*, 2003–2004, pp. 427–440.

15 *Runes. An Introduction*, op. cit., p. 11.

However, only four runes are identical or extremely close to north Italic letters: u, a, s and l. Borrowing could be plausible for the k, z/R, t and o runes, but the f, r, b, e and m runes are closer to Latin. Moreover, some letters remain without equivalents: þ (Þ), g (X), n (†), j (◊), ï (∫), p (K̊), ŋ (◊) and d (M̊). "There are still shapes whose genesis is hard to explain," writes Alain Marez, "because they match neither Latin nor north Italic alphabets."[16] There are also a lack of phonetic similarities between runes and north Italic letters, even when their shapes are quite similar, and this must be taken into account. For instance, the rune d and the italic letter s have more or less the same shape, but not the same phonetic value. The same goes with the runic l and the italic p, etc. Lastly, the letters of north Italic alphabets don't have names: just like Latin letters, they were only called by the sound their sound.

Another issue is the lack of a uniform model for the runes. In order to explain that the *Fuþark* was derived from north Italic writings, it is necessary to claim that the creators of runic writing did not borrow from a single alphabet, but from three or four different alphabets, which is not very plausible, especially since some "inventions" from unknown sources were also supposedly added. Wolfgang Krause himself acknowledges that "a precise model for the runes among north Etruscan alphabets has yet to be discovered."[17] Furthermore, the theory is weakened by the fact that no runic inscription prior to the 5th century has been found in southern Germany.

As we have seen earlier in this section, the supporters of the north Italic theory also fail to agree on which Germanic populations committed the borrowing. Marstrander and then Wolfgang Krause believed it was the Marcomanni, Helmut Arntz, Franz Altheim and Catherine Trautmann believed it was the Cimbri. Some other authors believed it was some "Germans from the Alps" (but that idea has been discredited) or that it was some Germanic soldiers that served in the Roman army, but these are merely suppositions. In fact, we could argue that the Cimbri were too busy to invent a writing after their defeat in 101 BC. Besides, why would they not have picked up the Greek or Latin alphabets anyway?

---

16   Alain Marez, *Anthologie runique*, Belles Lettres, Paris 2007, pp. 27–28.

17   *Les runes*, op. cit., p. 43.

11

The Contribution of Linguistics

MOST RUNOLOGISTS ARE RELUCTANT to admit that runic writing could have been created before Christ. That is because runology has been almost exclusively based on archaeology for a long time. Elmer H. Antonsen doesn't hesitate to write that "the conviction that runic writing came into being relatively late isn't grounded in science."[1] Linguists are more prone to believe that runic writing appeared earlier because they mainly rely on the epigraphic and linguistic analyses of the oldest inscriptions. Lucien Musset could still write in 1965 that "concerted efforts to study the phonetic and grammatical sources of runes are out of the ordinary."[2] It is not the case today.

The linguists that examine inscriptions in the Old *Fuþark* mainly focus on its "archaic" characteristics — which we have already described — like the fact that runes are written from right to left or in boustrophedon, which isn't the case for classical Greek or Latin from the imperial period. Antonsen writes that "those archaic traits which are typical of the oldest inscriptions can't be a coincidence and those inscriptions can't have been traced by 'primitive minds.'" Those traits must have been borrowed from the symbols of the alphabet when the borrowing from the writing system took place, which means that the runic alphabet could not have been inspired by the Romans

---

1   *Runes and Germanic Linguistics*, op. cit., p. 96.

2   *Introduction à la runologie*, op. cit., p. 69.

in the Rhine region since they wrote exclusively from left to right. Runic writing's appearance must have been prior to the oldest inscriptions that we know and of by a large margin, and it must have come into being much before the Roman occupation of the Rhine, and other aspects of the writing system go in the same direction."[3]

For instance, the fact that early runic writing had two different letters to express the /i/ sound: i and ī (| and ʃ, *eisaz and *iwaz) shows that the *Fuþark* could not have been invented later than the 2nd century, a time when the /ei/ diphthong of the common German was still different from the original /i/ diphthong, that is to say when non-accented diphthongs still existed as diphthongs. That is why we can find some -*ai* (instead of -*ei*) archaic diphthong endings in non-accented syllables in several ancient runic inscriptions (*anahahai* on the stone of Möjebro, *talgidai* on the fibula of Nøvling).[4]

Richard L. Morris, who also rejects the north Italic hypothesis for phonetic reasons, compared the runic tradition with the Mediterranean epigraphic traditions.

> The similarities between the runic writing system and the Greek or archaic Latin systems have up until now been ignored or simply asserted to be the result of imperfect attempts by primitive Germanic population to master the epigraphy of the highly refined classical traditions of imperial Rome and Hellenistic Greece. But when the runic tradition and the Mediterranean traditions at their first stages of development are put side by side, the results are extremely different […] the question 'where do the runes come from?' is yet to be answered because the defining traits of the archaic Greek and Latin alphabets were not sufficiently taken into consideration.[5]

Morris believes that it is necessary to compare the runes not only with the classical Greek alphabet, but also with the prior archaic Greek alphabets

---

3   *Runes and Germanic Linguistics*, op. cit. p. 111.

4   See Elmer H. Antonsen, "Die ältesten Runeninschriften in heutiger Sicht," in Heinrich Beck (ed.), *Germanenprobleme in heutiger Sicht*, Walter de Gruyter, Berlin 1986, pp. 321–343 (ici p. 338).

5   Richard L. Morris, *Runic and Mediterranean Epigraphy*, Odense University Press, Odense 1988, p. 2. See also the author's theory, *Umbilicus runicus. Runic and Mediterranean Epigraphy*, University of Illinois, Urbana 1983.

because the runes look more like the letters of the latter. Beyond the fact that both systems allow writing from right to left and in boustrophedon, they have more in common: they both ignore double consonants, they tend to remove the nasalized consonants before other consonants (for example a m before a b, or a n before a d or before a g), etc. By drawing comparisons between the *Fuþark* and primitive Greek alphabets that were gone by the 4th century BC, Morris obviously alludes to a borrowing that happened before to that time. He concludes that the study of runic and Mediterranean epigraphies "demonstrates that the resemblance of runic tradition with Greek and archaic Latin makes it impossible for the runes to have been borrowed from the Latin tradition around the birth of Christ — including the Latin tradition in Gaul and Germania — or from Greek from that same period. Around the time Christ was born, those alphabets had already been so stylized that if a borrowing happened that late, then the runes would have looked much more like the Greek or Latin alphabets of that time. And if the runes were borrowed then, then the first people to use the runes should have written from left to right because it was the only regular way to do it."[6]

Elmer H. Antonsen, whose approach (the structuralist type) is centered around the phonological system, sides with the opinion of his student Richard L. Morris according to whom runic writing was necessarily created before Christ, even if we have no material evidence for it. Antonsen writes: "Runic writing must have been considerably older than the first inscriptions we know about."[7] Moreover, he's virulently opposed to Erik Moltke's

---

6 Ibid., pp. 157–158.

7 Elmer H. Antonsen, "Zum Ursprung und Alter der germanischen Fuþarks," in Kurt R. Jankowsky and Ernst Dick (ed.), *Festschrift für Karl Schneider*, John Benjamins, Amsterdam 1982, pp. 3–15. By the same author: "The Graphemic System and the Germanic *Fuþark*," in Herbert Penzl, Irmengard Rauch and Gerald F. Carr (ed.), *Linguistic Method. Essays in Honor of Herbert Penzl*, Mouton, The Hague 1978, pp. 287–297; "On the Notion of 'Archaicizing' Inscriptions," in John Weinstock (ed.), *The Nordic Languages and Modern Linguistics*, University of Texas, Austin 1978, pp. 282–288; "The Oldest Runic Inscriptions in the Light of New Finds and Interpretations," *in Runor och runinskrifter. Föredrag vid Riksantikvarieämbetets och Vitterhetsakademiens symposium 8-11 september 1985*, Alkqvist & Wiksell International, Stockholm 1987, pp. 17–28; "On Runological and Linguistic Evidence for Dating Runic Inscriptions," art. cit. Antonsen's theories were criticized by Lena Pederson and Klaus Düwel, but Michael P. Barnes thinks those critics were "too hasty" ("What Is Runology, and Where Does It Stand Today?," in *Futhark. International Journal of Runic Studies*, 4, 2013, p. 24).

Latin theory which, according to him, has absolutely no basis. He also sees no reason to believe that runic writing appeared near Roman *limes* or that Celtic populations were an intermediary in their propagation. It could have just as well been spread by sea, he observes, since trade between Rome and Northern Europe was done by land or by sea.

Another discussion related to this debate is the dialectal status of the language written down as inscriptions in Old *Fuþark*. The language of the oldest inscriptions is commonly believed to be *urnordisch*, *altnordisch* or *spӓturnordisch*, meaning the state of the language prior to linguistic innovations that took place around 500, a state that still involves vocalism in the endings of words. Ottar Grønvik, Wolfgang Krause or Erik Moltke are among the supporters of this "Proto-Nordic" theory, whereas Enver A. Makaev confines himself to talk of a "runic Koine,"[8] and Robert Nedoma of "old-runic." However, it makes sense to believe that the older the first inscriptions are, the more the language they represent is close to the common Germanic language. Elmer H. Antonsen is one of those who think that those inscriptions correspond to a language closer to "Proto-Germanic" than "Proto-Nordic," because the Old *Fuþark* demonstrates a phonological system that can only be found in the *Urgermanisch* period.[9] That opinion, which was already held by Hans Kuhn and then Gustav Indrebø, is shared by Paolo Ramat. Hans Frede Nielsen believes that "old runic" resembles the northwestern Germanic language or even late the common Germanic language, but he thinks that most inscriptions in the Old *Fuþark* denote a language already somewhat close to Old Norse.[10] Lastly, we still have to

---

8   Enver A. Makaev, *The Language of the Oldest Runic Inscriptions. A Linguistic and Historical-Philological Analysis*, Kungl. Vitterhets historie och antikvitets akademien, Stockholm 1996.

9   "Die ältesten Runeninschriften in heutiger Sicht," art. cit.; *Runes and Germanic Linguistics*, op. cit., pp. 3–13 and 93–117. See also *A Concise Grammar of the Older Runic Inscriptions*, Max Niemeyer, Tübingen 1975, in which the author offers etymologies that are sometimes noticeaby different from those put forth by Hans Krahe or Wolfgang Krause (*Die Sprache der urnordischen Runeninschriften*, Carl Winter, Heidelberg 1971).

10 Hans Frede Nielsen, *The Early Runic Language of Scandinavia. Studies in Germanic Dialect Geography*, Carl Winter, Heidelberg 2000, p. 381. From the same author, see also "The Linguistic Status of the Early Runic Inscriptions of Scandinavia," in Klaus Düwel (Hg.), *Runeninschriften als Quellen interdisziplinäre Forschung*, op. cit., pp.

figure out whether the oldest runic inscriptions were written in the same language or in the same dialectal variant.

"We still don't exactly know whence [runic writing] came," writes Elmer H. Antonsen,

> but the pieces of evidence we have got indicate an archaic Mediterranean writing with Greek or Latin origins. The fact that Latin writing was itself inherited from Greek makes it virtually impossible to ascertain which one was more directly responsible for the appearance of the *Fuþark* [...] We aren't currently capable (and we probably never will be) to identify a specific local Mediterranean alphabet that produced the runes. The only thing we know is that the *Fuþark* is derived from the great archaic Greek tradition of writing like the Latin alphabet.[11]

Aage Kabell,[12] who believes that the origins of the runes are to be found in an archaic Greek alphabet, suggested in those circumstances to reexamine Isaac Taylor's old theory, which dares to purport that the runic alphabet comes from a Thracian alphabet from the 6th century BC.[13] Some of that theory was previously picked up by George Hempl.[14] Of course Klaus Düwel

---

539–555; "The Early Runic Inscriptions and Germanic Historical Linguistics," in Marie Stoklund, Michael Lerche Nielsen, Bente Holmberg and Gillian Fellows-Jensen (ed.), Runes and their Secrets, op. cit.; "The Grouping of the Germanic Languages and the Dialectal Provenance of the Oldest Runic Inscriptions of Scandinavia (AD 160–500)," in Oliver Grimm and Alexandra Pesch (Hg.), *Archäologie und Runen. Fallstudien zu Inschriften im älteren Futhark*, Wachholtz-Murmann, KielHamburg 2015, pp. 45–58. Frede Nielsen explains that "the idiom of the oldest runic inscriptions in Scandinavia is the most archaic one out of all of the confirmed Germanic languages." For a more general discussion, see Alfred Bammesberger and Gaby Waxenberger (Hg.), *Das "Fuþark" und seine einzelsprachlichen Weiterentwicklungen. Akten der Tagung in Eichstätt vom 20.–24. Juli 2003*, Walter de Gruyter, Berlin 2006.

11 *Runes and Germanic Linguistics*, op. cit., p. 116.
12 "Periculum runicum," art. cit.
13 Isaac Taylor, *Greeks and Goths. A Study on the Runes*, Macmillan, London 1879.
14 George Hempl, "The Origin of the Runes," in *Journal of English and Germanic Philology*, 1899, pp. 370–374; "The Runes and the Germanic Shift," in *Journal of English and Germanic Philology*, 1902, pp. 70–75. Theo Vennemann recently tried to explain some runes like ᚲ (p), ᛋ (i), ᛗ (e) or ᛟ (o), as a result of a borrowing from a Punic or Neo-punic alphabet from the 3rd or 2nd century BC, notably because the first letter of the Carthaginian alphabet is a f, like in the *Fuþark*. That theory, which is

objects to that "hyper archaic" theory that it's surprising that not a single inscription from that 500-year-long period (between the 6th and 1st century BC) was found.[15] Is that a decisive argument? Once again, runologists face the question of the preservation of the first inscriptions.

---

historiographically interesting, is nevertheless obviously problematic when it comes to its chronology (and how the alphabet spread). See Theo Vennemann, "Germanische Runen und phönizisches Alphabet," in *Sprachwissenschaft*, 2006, pp. 367–429; "Vowels in Punic and in Runic," in *Sprachwissenschaft*, 2013, pp. 265–280; "The Origin of the p Rune," ibid., pp. 281–286.

15 Klaus Düwel, Morris's recension in *Germania*, 1991, pp. 230–234.

12

Provisional Appraisal

There are many theories on when runic writing was created and on who created it. Most of them contradict each other or are incompatible with each other. There is no consensus. Why didn't the Germanic people use the Greek, Latin (or Etruscan) alphabet instead of creating their own writing from Greek, Latin or Etruscan?[1] And especially, why did they feel the need to completely disrupt the writing system they borrowed from Mediterranean people? Why take only a part of their alphabet and add signs from an unknown source to it? Why did they completely change the order of the letters they borrowed? Why did they group them into three distinct groups (the *ættir*)? Why did they give a name to every letter in accordance with the principle of acronyms?

The Phoenician, Greek, Latin, Etruscan or north Italic alphabets are all comprised of a sequence of letters, and all those sequences are virtually always in the same order, beside a few variations. It never crosses the mind of the people who inherit an anterior alphabet to change the inner workings of its order. Moreover, all those alphabets are composed of a continuous sequence of letters, without any sort of grouping like the *ættir*, so why didn't the *Fuþark* follow that pattern. It bears repeating that none of the theories

---

[1] As Lucien Musset wrote, "If Denmark had directly imitated a Mediterranean writing in the 1st or 2nd century AD, there would have been no reason to address any other source beside Latin writing (or maybe a Greek writing)" (*Introduction à la runologie*, op. cit., p. 33).

explain the peculiar order of the *Fuþark* or the division of the letters into three *ættir*.

Some runes are identical with Latin, Greek or north Italic letters when it comes to their shape and phonetic values. Some other runes are much more random, or even dubious. Anyways, there are always some runes with no equivalent (like ᛇ, ᛈ or ᛢ). We have to believe that they came from somewhere else, but where?[2] Whatever the answer, the *Fuþark* cannot be explained as a whole by a derivation or a borrowing from a single anterior writing system. In any case, runologists can only note reorganizations, additions, removals or modifications that they cannot account for.

If runic writing came from a Mediterranean alphabet, then it would be reasonable to assume that the oldest runic inscriptions would be found in southern Europe. Yet, it is completely the opposite: most of them are in northern Germany and in the Scandinavian peninsula, especially Denmark.[3] In other words, the more one goes south, the less inscriptions are to be found, and the more one goes north, the more inscriptions there are.[4] But this does not mean that the system is native to that region. Runic writing could very well have been invented in a meridional region and then have taken hold in Denmark and the neighboring territories after it spread there. Likewise, the objects bearing runic inscriptions that were found in Denmark could have been engraved somewhere else (especially since inscriptions do not necessarily have to be from the same historical period as the objects they are engraved on). Nonetheless, it is surprising that a

---

[2] Let us mention just for the anecdote the theory that runic writing's origin was partially Nabataean, which was put forth by John Troeng ("A Semitic Origin of Some Runes. An Influential Foreign Presence in Denmark c. AD 200," in *Fornvännen*, 2003, pp. 289–305), and let's not forget Örjan Svensonn's theory, which asserts that the runes were derived from the Aramaic language and that they are a "coded" writing emanating from one of the ancient "lost tribes" of Israel (*De blekingska runornas hemligheter*, the author, Karlskrona 2001)!

[3] While referring to Erik Moltke's work, Lucien Musset writes that "it is quite likely that Denmark was one of the first centres of Old *Fuþark*, if not the first one" (*Introduction à la runologie*, op. cit., p. 31). See also Michael P. Barnes, Runes. *A Handbook*, Boydell Press, Woodbridge 2012, p. 9.

[4] Wolfgang Krause underlines that "the absence of ancient runic writing inscriptions in the southern Germanic area should not be attributed to the fact that wood is a material that perishes fast. This is not an admissible argument. Indeed, we know of a whole lot of runic inscriptions inscribed in wood from the North" (*Les runes*, op. cit., p. 53).

writing that is supposed to have been created by coming into contact with Mediterranean populations left so few traces in the areas where that contact is supposed to have taken place. Since Denmark is 1100 kilometers away from the Mediterranean as the crow flies, we have to figure out who brought runic writing north, as well as in what form and under what conditions. It is generally assumed that the runes spread north by land, by following the Rhine and the Neckar valley, near current Württemberg, or by an Italy-Bohemia/Moravia-Denmark route. Musset notes that "thanks to archaeology, we know that it's quite possible that alphabetical texts spread North."[5] Even more so since northern Europe and southern Europe have been in contact much before Christ, if only because of the routes formed since the Bronze Age to trade amber.[6] But then again, specialists still disagree. None of the hypotheses raised so far are confirmed by substantial evidence.

Whether runic writing was invented by a single person or a group (of "merchants," of "priests," of "warriors" etc.) remains controversial as well. A borrowing from a Mediterranean alphabet obviously assumes that at least one Germanic language speaker could also speak and read the Mediterranean language that the alphabet transcribed. That means that that person was at some point in physical contact with the people that spoke the language. Many peoples are believed to have been the ones who spread it: the Goths from the banks of the Vistula (Akeber) or from the Black Sea (von Friesen), the Cimbri and the Teutons from the Transpadane region (Baseche, Altheim-Trautmann), the Marconni from Bohemia and the Quadi (Marstrander, Krause), the Heruli (Höfler), or even some Celtic intermediaries. Those claims remain just hypotheses.

---

5   *Introduction à la runologie*, op. cit., p. 39.

6   The Greeks from the west part of the Mediterranean Sea were already in contact with Scandinavia around 300 BC. We also know that the amber found in Mycenaean tombs had Danish origins. On the ancient "amber routes," see J. M. de Navarro, "Prehistoric Routes between Northern Europe and Italy Defined by the Amber Trade," in *The Geographical Journal*, December 1925, pp. 481–507; Arnold S. Spekke, *Ancient Amber Routes and the Discovery of the Eastern Baltic*, M. Goppers, Stockholm 1957; Patty C. Rice, *Amber. The Golden Gem of the Ages*, Van Nostrand Reinhold, New York 1980; Gisela Graichen and Alexander Hesse (ed.), *Die Bernsteinstraße. Verborgene Handelswege zwischen Ostsee und Nil*, Rowohlt, Reinbek bei Hamburg 2012.

All the theories that suggest a borrowing later than the 2nd century (like the one that relies on Goths from the Black Sea) have to be dropped for chronological reasons, since we now know of inscriptions prior to that period. It is obvious that runic writing can not have been created in southern Europe at a time when it was already being used in northern Germany or Scandinavia. If runic writing was already used in the 1st century AD, then it's unlikely that it was derived from Hellenistic Greek or Latin. Conversely, it would be more likely that it came from the North Italic alphabets (or the archaic Greek alphabets).

It is also quite daring to explain the creation of an alphabet from not one, but several sources (other alphabets). Whereas Ludwig F. A. Wimmer suggested to tie the runes only to the Latin alphabet, Bugge, von Friesen, Marstrander and Hammarström suggested tying it to several writing systems: to create the *Fuþark*, some letters were supposedly borrowed from an alphabet, and then some other letters were borrowed from another alphabet, and some more from a third alphabet. Psychologically speaking, the theory that the *Fuþark* was created by his inventor by picking some letters from different alphabets and mixing them with letters of his own creation is tenuous. Musset reckons that "the idea of drawing inspiration from several writing systems is not absurd," but he admits that this idea "has been an insurmountable obstacle for many runologists."[7]

Moreover, not only the letters' shapes but also their phonological values must be taken into account. Too often we forget that "in an alphabet of the geometric kind, the number of stroke and curve combinations is quite limited, so letters cannot be seriously considered to have been borrowed or to be related unless they have enough in common not only when it comes to their signs, but also when it comes to the sounds they express."[8]

As early as 1874, Ludwig F. A. Wimmer laid down the principle that if both the shape and the phonetic value of a rune matches that of a letter from Mediterranean alphabets, we can conclude that the rune is derived from the letter. But there is an issue with that principle when it is applied to

---

7 *Introduction à la runologie*, op. cit., p. 48.
8 Lucien Musset, ibid., p. 42. From that viewpoint, one can only reject Henrik Williams' opinion, according to whom "only the form determines the origin of the runes' forms" ("The Origin of the Runes," art. cit., p. 214).

the whole alphabet, because the likeness of shapes is not always linked with the phonological equivalence. For instance, the rune ᚹ resembles the Latin P or the Greek *rho*, but it denotes the sound /w/, but it's the rune ᛈ which denotes the sound /p/. Why does the rune ᛟ express the sound /o/, whereas the rune ◊ which is close to the Latin O expresses the sound /ng/? Why is it that the rune ᛃ expresses the sound /j/ when the rune ᛉ, which is close to the Latin Y, expresses the sound /z/? If we go by the derivation or borrowing theory, the discrepancies between letters, phonemes and sounds are hard to explain.

If we assume that the first runic inscriptions have an archaic character that alludes to the primitive stages of classical Mediterranean alphabets, that primitive character evidently removes the possibility of a derivation that took place in the classical period. Thus, runic writing must be more related to the north Italic alphabets than the Greek and Latin alphabets. However, we are certain that runic writing is even more related to archaic Greek alphabets, which are the forebears of the Italic alphabets.

David N. Parsons believes that there is actually "very little evidence that the runes were developed incrementally from an anterior alphabet," but "different characteristics of that writing give us reason to believe that the inscriptions that survived were derived from a well established system that was especially well suited to the requirements of the Germanic language."[9] "We simply don't know without a doubt where the runes come from," writes Richard L. Morris, who adds that "estimating that the runes cannot be older than the birth of Christ, not only makes one base his theory on elements that aren't backed by enough evidence, but it also leads one towards fallacious interpretations of the inscriptions themselves."[10] Elmer H. Antonsen goes further: "Without delving into the details of all the theories on the origin of [the runes], we can know one thing for sure: none of them fulfill adequately enough the requirements set by the researchers to be the final solution to that question. In other words, runologists have yet to identify

---

9   David N. Parsons, *Recasting the Runes. The Reform of the Anglo-Saxon"Fuþorc,"* Institutionen för nordiska språk, Uppsala universitet, Uppsala 1999, p. 15.
10 *Runic and Mediterranean Epigraphy*, op. cit., p. 1.

with meaningful certainty a specific Mediterranean alphabet as the source of the *Fuþark*."[11]

The main hypotheses on the origin of runic writing have something in common: they all are based only on chronological arguments. Since there is no proof that runic writing was present before the birth of Christ, then it is argued that it can only come from a writing that was present before the birth of Christ. But a derivation or a borrowing is not the only way to explain relatedness. Relatedness can come from a common heritage that sprang parallel evolutions, like it often occurs in linguistic evolutions. In this perspective, runic signs would be derived from a single European symbolic system that was already in use in protohistory, and the Mediterranean alphabets would also be derived from that system (maybe Ogham as well). That's a bold hypothesis, but it deserves to be investigated further. That is what we are going to do now.

---

11 *Runes and Germanic Linguistics*, op. cit., p. 93.

THE GREAT RUNESTONE OF JELLING. It was erected in 983 by the son and successor of the king Gorm III, Harald Bluetooth, in memory of his parents and to celebrate his conquest of Norway and Denmark. Denmark offered a replica to the city of Rouen in 1911 to commemorate the one thousandth anniversary of the Treaty of Saint-Clair-sur-Epte.

AN ILLUSTRATED STONE from the island of Gotland (8th century). It represents the welcome of warriors in the Valhöll (Valhalla). In the top right corner: Oðhinn — Wodan riding his eight-legged horse, Sleipnir.

THE RUNESTONE OF TUNE (Norway), dates back to around 450.
It was discovered in 1867 on the shore of the Oslo gulf.

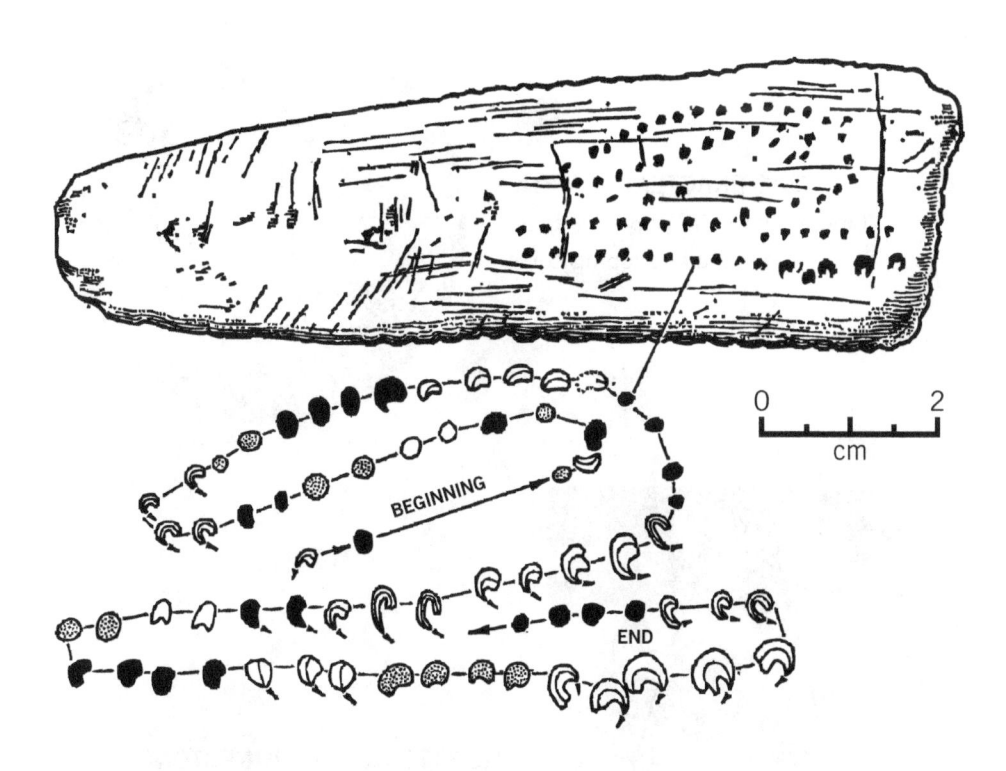

SLAB FROM THE BLANCHARD SHELTER (Dordogne) and dating to the Aurignacian (−35 000 years). According to Alexander Marshack, the sixty-nine marks in the shape of circles or crescents correspond to different phases of the moon.

THE RUNIC INSCRIPTION of Nordhuglen.

THE BRACTEATE OF FYN. It represents a bird of prey, a divine figure and a galloping horse.

THE YTTERGÄRDE RUNESTONE'S INSCRIPTION. It was most likely engraved in the second quarter of the 11th century. It is read from right to left (starting from the snake's head), and then from left to right. It commemorates a Swedish viking named Ulf.

THE FAMOUS RAMSUNGBERG RUNESTONE. Its length is 4.8 meters. It depicts the legend of Sigurd.

KNIFE HANDLE made of bone bearing the runic inscription "latam hari."

A page from the "Codex runicus."

THE SMALL DANISH VILLAGE NAMED JELLING, near the city of Bejly, in Jutland. There are two burial mounds and two monolithic runestones that have different sizes there. This is the bigger one. The second one was erected by the king Gorm the Old, dead in 958, in memory of his wife Thyra.

BRACTEATE FOUND IN 1774 in Vadstena (Östergötland) listing the runes of the *Fuþark*.

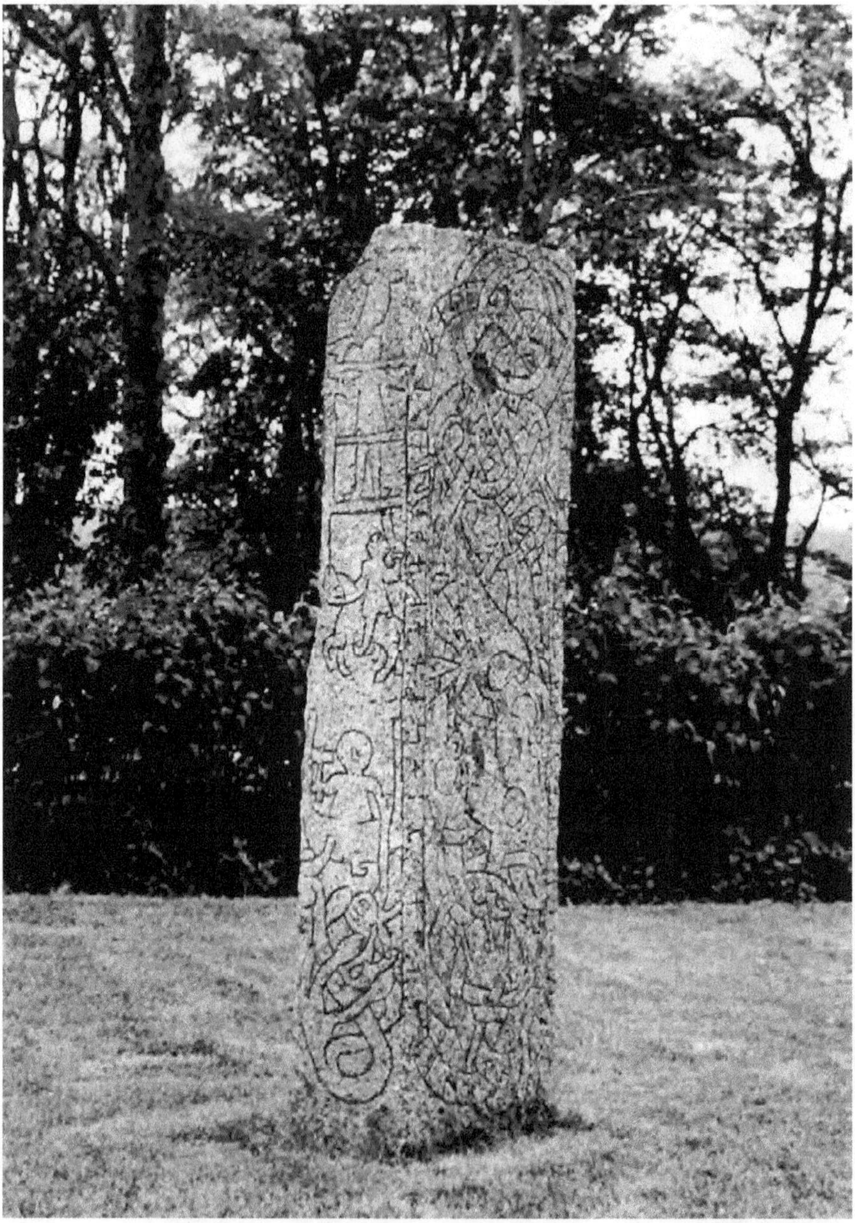

PART II

13

Attempts at Explanation

As we have already pointed out: the first runic inscriptions present a system that is already perfectly stabilized. All runologists agree on that. Maurice Cahen writes that "We agree to accept that the order and the division of the runic alphabet were set around the time it was created: given how all the other Germanic alphabets are, it must date back to ancient times."[1] Lucien Musset writes that One of the most remarkable characteristics of the *Fuþark* is its relative flexity."[2] David N. Parsons writes about the *Fuþark* that it "*goes back to the earliest days of the scripti.*" "Since the very first inscriptions," writes Wolfgang Krause, "runic writing appears everywhere under a definitively set form."[3] "One thing is unquestionable: since the first monuments, it [the *Fuþark*] appears under its final form and in its immutable order that is also present in half a dozen inscriptions from the 4th to the 6th centuries," writes Alain Marez.[4] The oldest inscriptions do not display a system that is being formed. It is already complete at the beginning.

The same goes for the peculiar order of the *Fuþark* and for the division of the letters into three eight-letter groups. "The order of the runes and its tripartite distribution within the sequence seem to be ancient, that may date back to the

---

1 "Origine et développement de l'écriture runique," art. cit., p. 16.
2 *Introduction à la runologie*, op. cit., p. 90.
3 *Les runes*, op. cit., p. 52 (see p. 52 above).
4 *Anthologie runique*, op. cit., p. 33.

creation of system,"⁵ writes Alain Marez. The reason behind the division into three *ættir* remains unknown. But we should keep in mind that the Icelandic word *ætt* derives from the name of the number "eight" according to Magnus Olsen, which makes some sense since it refers to an sequence of eight signs.⁶

Many studies were conducted on the names of the runes, the most monumental one was Karl Schneider's.⁷ Two theories arose to try to explain the order of the *Fuþark's* runes from their names. One by trying to connect it with some kind of mnemonic poem, which is not very credible (everybody can memorize the order of the letters of a twenty-four sign alphabet), the other by noticing that most runes can be sorted in antithetical pairs, which is more interesting: "cattle" (**fehu*) and "aurochs" (**ūruz*), "giant" (**þurisaz*) and "Asa" (ferula) (**ansuz*), etc. That idea that the system brings together runes with opposite or complementary meanings in couples was first brought up by Erik Brate,⁸ and then it was picked up in different ways by Friedrich von der Leyen, Elmar Seebold⁹ and Bernard Mees. Karl Schneider believes that the names of the runes were divided into four main groups, and that the concepts they expressed were assembled in pairs. Nonetheless, that approach remains speculative, like Wolfgang Jungandreas' (who supports the Latin theory) attempt to explain the names of the runes by taking into account cosmological elements.¹⁰

---

5   Ibid., p. 24.

6   One must note that Terje Spurkland is the author of a controversial theory according to which the total number of signs in a row of runes should have originally been eight. See Terje Spurkland, *Norwegian Runes and Runic Inscriptions*, op. cit., p. 80.

7   Karl Schneider, *Die germanischen Runennamen. Versuch einer Gesamtdeutung*, Anton Hain, Meisenheim am Glan 1956. See also Wolfgang Krause, "Untersuchungen zu den Runennamen I," in *Nachrichten der Akademie der Wissenschaften in Göttingen, Philologisch-Historische Klasse*, 1946-1947, pp. 60-63; "Untersuchungen zu den Runennamen II," ibid., 1948, pp. 93-108; Robert Nedoma, "Runennamen," in Heinrich Beck, Dieter Geuenich and Heiko Steuer (ed.), *Reallexikon der Germanischen Altertumskunde*, vol. 25, Walter de Gruyter, Berlin 2003, pp. 556-560.

8   Erik Brate, "Runradens ordningsfjöljd," in *Arkiv for nordisk filologi*, 1920, pp. 193-207.

9   Elmar Seebold, "Was haben die Germanen mit den Runen gemacht? Und wieviel haben sie davon von ihren antiken Vorbildern gelernt?," in Bela Brogyani and Thomas Krömmelbein (ed.), *Germanic Dialects. Linguistic and Philologic Investigations*, Benjamins, Amsterdam 1986, pp. 525-583.

10 Wolfgang Jungandreas, "Die Namen der Runen. Fuþark und Kosmologie," in *Onoma*, 1974, pp. 365-390. For a critique of that viewpoint, see Edgar C. Polomé, "The Names of the Runes," art. cit.

Starting from 1927, Sigurd Agrell developed speculations that were even more audacious. He argued that every letter represented a number, like in Hebrew Gematria, and that those numbers had magic attributes based on the names of the runes. He supported the Greek theory, but he also believed the creators of runic writing were Germanic soldiers who served the Roman Empire and were initiated into Mithras' mysteries in the Rhineland. Since the rune *ūruz, u (ᚢ) means "aurochs, bull" (we know that bulls were central in Mithraism), he argued that the Fuþark was actually a "uþark," because some runic wizards allegedly moved f (ᚠ) from the twenty-fourth and final spot to the first, in order to hide the key to their numeral mysticism from the uninitiated![11] That theory, which involved out-of-control mystical and numerological considerations, was popular in the early 1930s.[12] However it is completely forsaken nowadays because there's absolutely no reason to believe that the Fuþark was actually some "uþark," and because we know that the oldest runic inscriptions came into being much before the time Mithraism spread to Germania. In spite of this, that theory was picked up in the 1970s by Heinz Klingenberg.[13]

Another ingenious but just as improbable explanation of the peculiar order of the letters of the Fuþark was brought up by Murray K. Dahm.[14] Based on Polybius's (2nd century BC) and Sextus Julius Africanus's (beginning of the 3rd century) accounts, he reminds people that there were fortifications and towers on Roman borders that were used to send messages by lighting torches, sort of like semaphores. According to him, the Romans divided their alphabets into three eight-letter groups and brandished torches in coded directions and in a coded rhythm to send their messages. That hypothesis obviously involves a derivation of runic writing from Latin. But we

---

11 Sigurd Agrell, *Runornas talmystik och dess antika förebild*, Lund 1927; *Zur Frage nach dem Ursprung der Runennamen*, Lund 1928; *Die spätantike Alphabetmystik und die Runenreihe*, Lund 1931–32; "Die Herkunft der Runenschrift," in *Kunglinga humanistika vetenskapssamfundet i Lund*, 1937–1938, pp. 65–117.

12 See in particular Franz Rolf Schröder, *Altgermanische Kulturprobleme*, Walter de Gruyter, Berlin 1929.

13 Heinz Klingenberg, *Runenschrift — Schriftdenken — Runeninschriften*, Carl Winter, Heidelberg 1973.

14 Murray K. Dahm, "Roman Frontier Signalling and the Order of the 'Fuþark'," in *The Journal of Indo-European Studies*, spring-summer 2011, pp. 1–12.

don't have much information on the exact nature of the signals and most importantly why would the inventors of runic writing have changed the order of the Latin alphabet for that rather marginal way?

The runes' names were also studied etymologically and by examining their position within the *Fuþark*. Another question that was asked was whether the *Fuþark* came before or after every rune got a name, as it would let us know whether their names gave them their position within the "alphabet." According to that hypothesis, which was also picked up by Helmut Arntz, the runes' names not only refer to words, but also to symbols expressed by those words, and those symbols could be linked to an ancient solar cult that is characteristic of a people chiefly composed of farmers (maybe the Vanir in the Germanic religion, in opposition to the Æsir). Wolfgang Krause also believed that the runes' names were linked to the the gods' realm.[15] That line of reasoning implies that the runes are not only used as phonemes, but also as symbols, giving us reason to believe that their use came prior to the creation of runic writing.

We shall retain this hypothesis because it is the only one that explains the peculiar order of the *Fuþark* and maybe even the distribution of runes into three *ættir*. The runes, used previously for religious, magical, oracular and divinatory purposes supposedly turned into a writing through contact with an alphabet from Mediterranean cultures whose letters were somewhat similar to them. But they should have conserved their original order and their division in three sequences that are eight runes long. Their names could be another proof of their use before they were used for writing. Therefore, runic writing would supposedly be the result of the fusion of an alphabetical writing with symbolic signs previously used.

Wolfgang Krause precisely offered to make the distinction between the *Lautrunen* and the *Begriffsrunen*, the runes used as sounds or phonemes and the runes used as symbols or concepts.[16] As phonemes, runes derive

---

15 See also Sigmund Feist, "Die religionsgeschichtliche Bedeutung der ältesten Runeninschriften," in *Journal of English and Germanic Philology*, 1922, pp. 602–611.

16 See Wolfgang Krause, *Runeninschriften im älteren Fuþark*, Max Niemeyer, Halle/Saale 1937, p. 4. See also *Was man in Runen ritzte*, Max Niemeyer, Halle/Saale 1935; "Die Runen als Begriffszeichen," in Kurt Helmut Schlottig (ed.), *Beiträge zur Runenkunde und nordischen Sprachwissenschaft. Gustav Neckel zu seinem 60. Geburtstag dargebracht*, Otto Harrassowitz, Leipzig 1938, pp. 35–53 (picked up in Wolfgang Krause,

from a North Italic alphabet, but as concepts, they derive from pre-runic symbols (*vorrunische Sinnbilder*) that date back to protohistory. "There was an extreme diversity of symbolic drawings wherever the Germanic language spread," writes Krause, "and much before the birth of runes. Therefore we are justified to ask whether the association of genuine runic characters with symbolic drawings of the same kind could explain in some way the irreducible shapes of runic characters through some formal filiation."[17] Some of those "symbolic drawings" can incidentally be found right next to "alphabetical" runes in inscriptions such as the Kowel spearhead, or on the rocks of Kårstad, Norway (5th century), and the Himmelstadlund in Sweden.

The concept of the *Begriffsrunen*, that is to say conceptual or ideographic runes, is obviously controversial. Klaus Düwel says that the notion needs to handled carefully (*Behutsamkeit*).[18]

"Before the appearance of a coherent *Fuþark*, there supposedly was in the Germanic world several manifestations of the use of signs that are more or less similar to runes, with an obvious symbolic value," reckons Lucien Musset, who nonetheless doesn't give much credit to that hypothesis.[19] While still remaining skeptical, he acknowledges that "nothing is in the way of seeing [in the runes] the legacy of some 'pre-runic signs' that were used all across the Germanic or Roman worlds as symbolic signs, recognition signs, oracular instruments, to certify property etc."[20]

Schriften zur Runologie und Sprachwissenschaft, Walter de Gruyter, Berlin 2014, pp. 150–165).

17 *Les runes*, op. cit., p. 50.

18 See Klaus Düwel, "Begriffsrunen," in Heinrich Beck, Herbert Jankuhn et al. (ed.), *Reallexikon der Germanischen Altertumskunde*, vol. 2, Walter de Gruyter, Berlin 1974, pp. 150–153.

19 *Introduction à la runologie*, op. cit., p. 41.

20 Ibid., p. 88.

14

Symbols and "Pre-Writings"

RUPESTRIAN SCANDINAVIAN ENGRAVINGS THAT mainly date to the second Nordic Bronze Age (1300–120 BC) and the transitory Iron Age period (800–600 BC) (*hällristningar*) were frequently used to try to identify graphic "pre-runic" signs. Those engravings, which were found in Tanum and Fossum in the Bohuslän province on the west coast of Sweden, as well as on the Bornholm Island, near Trondheim in southeastern Norway, are plentiful. 20,000 of them were found in Uppland, 24,000 in Västergötland, 15,000 in Östergötland and 12,000 in Södermanland.[1] Franz Altheim and Elizabeth Trautmann are some of those who rely on them to explain the origins of the runes.[2] But as seen earlier in this book, they also cite the engraved signs of the Val Camonica (Italy) that go back to the chalcolithic period and the beginning of the bronze age (1800–1500 BC). There again there's plenty of material since we have found upwards of 130,000 different engravings on the rocks of the Val Camonica and on the rocks of the Vallée des merveilles, which is situated on both sides of the Mont Bégo, in the Alpes-Maritimes.[3] Altheim and Trautmann believe

---

1   See Louritz Baltzer, *Hällristningar från Bohuslän — Glyphes des rochers du Bohuslän (Suède)*, Handelstidnings Aktiebolag, Göteborg 1881–1908; *Hällristningar och hällmålningar i Sverige*, Forums Bokförlag, Stockholm 1989.

2   *Vom Ursprung der Runen*, op. cit., p. 49.

3   The engravings of the Val Camonica were mostly studied by Emmanuel Anati, according to whom "rupestrian art is writing before writing" ("L'art rupestre est écriture avant l'écriture"), and the engravings of the Vallée des merveilles by Henry de Lumley.

that some of those signs are the sources of the runes that have no equivalent in Mediterranean alphabets.

But the rupestrian Scandinavian engravings as well as the engravings on the rocks of the Val Camonica are far from being the only ones that could be considered. In many cases, archaeological excavations brought to light signs and sequences of engraved signs not only in the territories of ancient Germanic (or Celtic) cultures, but also all over Europe. The oldest ones date back to the Upper Paleolithic.

Besides the engraved signs found in Glozel in 1924 that remain controversial, in spite of the suspicion that it was a plain and simple fake being now quelled,[4] there are the rupestrian engravings of La Madeleine, of Gourdan, of Font-de-Gaume, of the Eyzies, of the Cave of the Trois-Frères (Ariège), of the Cave of Lortet, the signs on the Roche Bertier which go back to the Magdalenian (around 10,000 BC) and on a pebble of the Cave of Puy Ravel in the Bourbonnais, the two hundred colorful pebbles bearing graphic signs found in 1889 in Mas d'Azil (Ariège), the marks on the Cave of Altamira's dome in Spain, the sequences of signs engraved on potteries that date back to the end of the bronze age that were found in Moras-en Valloire, the signs found in 1894 in the dolmenic chamber of Carrazedo, in the Alvão site (Portugal), that is supposedly about 8000 years old, etc.

All these signs that we obviously cannot decypher have been carefully accounted for. They are often referred to as "alphabetiforms" or "pre-writings,"[5] meaning that they were not really writing systems, but their

---

See Henry de Lumley, "Les gravures rupestres de l'âge du bronze de la Vallée des merveilles, Mont Bego, Alpes-Maritimes," in *L'Anthropologie*, 1984, 4, pp. 613–647; Daniel Riba, Les gravures rupestres *du Val Camonica*, France-Empire, Paris 1984. Emilia Masson also offered a deciphering.

4   See Nicole Torchet, Patrick Ferryn and Jacques Gossart, *L'affaire de Glozel. Histoire d'une controverse archéologique*, Copernic, Paris 1978; Alice Gérard, *Glozel. Les os de la discorde*, Temps présent, Paris 2013.

5   See Hans Jensen, *Die Schrift in Vergangenheit und Gegenwart*, Deutscher Verlag der Wissenschaften, Berlin 1969; Maxime Gorce, *Les pré-écritures et l'évolution des civilisations (18 000 à 8000 avant J.-C.)*, Klincksieck, Paris 1974; Károly Földes-Papp, *Von Felsbild zum Alphabet. Die Geschichte der Schrift von ihren früheste Vorstufen bis zur modernen lateinischen Schreibschrift*, Gondrom, Bayreuth 1975; Marthe Chollot-Varagnac, "Les origines du graphisme symbolique," *Essai d'analyse des écritures en préhistoire*, Fondation Singer-Polignac, Paris 1980; André Cherpillod, "L'écriture en

purpose was to convey something, and that they had a given signification for both the people who engraved them and the people who saw them. So, it seems like quite some pictographic and logographic signs have been used for symbolic representation or religious purposes since prehistory. The number of pre- and protohistoric signs that could have been used as inspiration for runes seems to be considerable, even if it is impossible to establish lineages between them.

Incidentally, in some cases it may not be just symbolic communication, but rather fully-fledged writing, or at least the "precursory stage of writing" (Emilia Masson). Thanks to radiocarbon dating, we now know that a writing was already in use in the beginning of the Neolithic in the Vinca and Karanovo cultures, in the Danube valley near Belgrade. That writing, which predates by a large margin the Sumerian pictograms (that didn't come into being before the end of the 4th millennium BC), was used from the end of the 6th millennium BC to around 3500 BC, meaning the arrival of Indo-Europeans in the region. M. A. Georgievsky started using it in 1940. Unlike ancient writing systems from the Orient (Egyptian hieroglyphs, Hittite and Luwian hieroglyphs, Sumerian cuneiform), it is a linear writing, which is apparently logographic (each sign conveys a concept) and non-phonographic (each sign conveys an individual sound or syllable). It only has 210 signs and some variations for thirty-six of them. The majority of the inscriptions found across thirty different sites are brief and present on ritual or votive objects. Unfortunately, they are hard to decipher as we know nothing about the spoken languages in the region before the arrival of the Indo-Europeans.[6]

Europe à l'époque préhistorique," in *Nouvelle Ecole*, 50, 1998, pp. 93–111; Alain Nicolas and Jean Combier, *Une écriture préhistorique? Le dossier archéologique de Moras-en-Valloire*, La Mirandole, Pont-Saint-Esprit 2009.

6   See Shan M. M. Winn, *Pre-Writing in Southeastern Europe. The Sign system of the Vinca Culture*, ca. 4000 BC, Western Publ., Calgary 1981; Emilia Masson, "L'écriture" dans les civilisations danubiennes néolithiques," in *Kadmos*, 1984, pp. 89–123; Richard Rudgley, *Lost Civilizations of the Stone Age*, Century, London 1998 (Chapter 4: "The Signs of Old Europe: Writing or Pre-Writing?," pp. 58–85); Michaël Guichard, "Les avant-courriers de l'écriture dans la vallée du Danube," in Anne-Marie Christin (ed.), *Histoire de l'écriture*, op. cit., pp. 25–27. Harald Haamann ("Writing from Old Europe to Ancient Crete — A Case of Cultural Continuity," in *The Journal of IndoEuropean*

Some other significant findings have been extracted from the Danube region and the Balkans. Some signs which look like letters laid out on four lines have been found in 1969 on the 6000- to 7000-year-old slab of clay of Gradesnica (western Bulgaria). The clay seal of Karanovo, found in 1968 near Stara Zagora, also in Bulgaria, dates back to around 3000 BC. The three tablets of Tartaria, found in 1963 by the Romanian prehistory specialist Ivan Vlassa near Turdas, Transylvania, also seem to bear primitive writing signs. We used to think for a long time that they were influenced by Sumerian writing, but now they are believed to be connected to the Cotofani culture. They supposedly date back to 4500 BC, and could therefore be anterior to the first civilizations of Mesopotamia.

Studies, Autumn-Winter 1989, pp. 251–275) links the writings of "Old Europe" with the linear writing of the Aegean, like the Cypro-Minoan Linear.

15

The Debate On "Magic"

THE OPPOSITION BETWEEN MAGIC and religion, which is a characteristic of Judeo-Christian monotheism, isn't present in European paganism, and they were even said to have an "essential similarity."[1] "In most Indo-European civilizations," writes François-Xavier Dillman, "magic definitely cannot be disassociated from all of the beliefs, representations, religious rites [...] on the contrary, it is one of the most prevalent components, one of those that resists the most against Christianization."[2] The same author underlines that runic writing and Germanic magic are often "one and the same."[3] Patrick Moisson also emphasizes that there is a fine line between magic and religion, but he notes that whereas religion seeks to conciliate divinities with sacrifice and worship, magic "constrains divine powers with appropriate rites," which assumes the existence of impersonal forces and "means to constrain the supernatural world."[4] Magic and religion are never brought into opposition like Good and Evil, or the authentic and

---

1 Haralds Biezais, *Von der Wesensidentität der Religion und Magie*, Åbo Akademi, Åbo 1978.

2 François-Xavier Dillmann, *Les magiciens dans l'Islande ancienne. Etudes sur la représentation de la magie islandaise et de ses agents dans les sources littéraires norroises*, Kungl. Gustav Adolfs Akademien för Svensk Folkkultur, Uppsala 2006, p. 12.

3 "Tripartition fonctionnelle et écriture runique en Scandinavie à l'époque païenne," art. cit., p. 250.

4 Patrick Moisson, "La polarité magie-religion dans le monde indoeuropéen," in *Etudes indo-européennes*, 1990, pp. 137–189.

the inauthentic, but rather are complementary aspects of holiness, which in Indo-European cultures are not brought into conflict.

The Old Norse term *taufr(ar)* first meant the wizardry or sorcery instruments, and then sorcery itself (see *töfrar* "seduction" in Icelandic). *Seiðr* is a specific kind of Norse magic which associates divination with sorcery (good or more often than not evil). It was mainly used in Scandinavia at the end of the Iron Age. Women seem to have been the only ones practicing its divinatory aspects. In Chapter 7 of the *Ynglinga Saga* which was written in 1230, Snorri Sturluson says that practicing *seiðr* is a shameful act for men (*karlmenn*). He also states in Chapter 4 that *seiðr* was first practiced by the Vanir divinities and then the Vanir goddess Freyja shared it to the Æsir gods, in particular Óðinn (*hon kenndi fyrst með Ásum seið, sem Vönum var títt*). In the *Lokasenna*, Loki reproaches Óðinn for practicing *seiðr*.

If the ancient Germanic peoples knew about the runes before they used them to write, such as when they used them for divination purposes for example, and if the runes kept some magical value as a figment of their previous use when they started using them for writing purposes, then the question surrounding "runic magic" obviously becomes essential. An immense amount of literature has been written on that topic, which fed a debate that was sometimes tumultuous.

Lucien Musset writes:

> One of the most controversial and essential questions of the history of runology is to know whether runes are only a writing, like the Latin alphabet, or whether they are signs whose value is primarily magical, whose main use was to convey incantations. Almost all major runologists agree since the beginning of the 20th century that the latter is true.[5]

The "magic" standpoint is indeed supported by many authors like Sophus Bugge, Magnus Olsen, Carl J. S. Marstrander, Emanuel Linderholm,[6] Hans Brix,[7] Jan de Vries (who calls runic writing *Zauberschrift*), Wolfgang Krause and many others. But it has also garnered detractors.

---

5   Lucien Musset, "Problèmes de runologie," in *Etudes germaniques*, 1957, p. 250–253, ici p. 250 (texte repris in *Nordica et Normannica*, Société des études nordiques, Paris 1997, p. 101).

6   Emanuel Linderholm, *Nordisk magi. I. Urnordisk magi*, P. A. Norstedt, Stockholm 1918.

7   Hans Brix, *Studier i nordisk runemagi*, Nordisk Forlag, København 1928.

Anders Bæksted is the author who is the most hostile to any "magic" interpretation. He wrote a consequential book[8] in 1952 which impressed many specialists, including Lucien Musset (who said he was "converted"). In that book, which can be considered to be hypercritical, Bæksted actually mostly takes on extreme opinions, like Magnus Olsen's who went as far as to claim that "the runes were not created for everyday life purposes, but rather to fulfill a supernatural mission,"[9] and gematrian or numerological interpretations that thrived as early as the end of the 19th century before being systematized by authors like Sigurd Agrell. The critique of "runic numerology" was then expanded by Wolfgang Morgenroth.[10] One can only side with him on that point.

Since then, the debate kept growing. Raymond I. Page calls the runologists who associate the runes with magic "inventive," and he calls the runologists who still don't want to hear anything about magic "skeptics."[11] Although he focuses his criticism on the Anglo-Saxon area, he puts himself into the "skeptic" category, along with Elmer H. Antonsen and Erik Moltke. Even if Antonsen acknowledges that it is "entirely possible" that one of the first purposes of the runes was magical, he still points out that until the 5th century, not one runic inscription that mentions a pagan divinity was found.[12] It is true, but it is not as significant as he leads us to believe, because the issue at hand is not religion, but magic: although there is no mention of the gods in the oldest runic inscriptions, all kinds of curses, spells and conjurations can be found. Erik Moltke goes further and thinks it is foolish to see any magical characteristic in the runes. Enver A. Makaev is of the same mind.

---

8 Anders Bæksted, *Målruner og troldruner. Runemagiske studier*, Gyldendal, København 1952.

9 Magnus Olsen, *Om troldruner*, Akademiska Bokhandeln, Uppsala 1917.

10 Wolfgang Morgenroth, "Zahlenmagie in Runeninschriften. Kritische Bemerkungen zu einigen Interpretationsmethoden," in *Wissenschaftliche Zeitschrift der Ernst-Moritz-Arndt Universität Greifswald*, 1961, pp. 279–283.

11 Raymond I. Page, "Anglo-Saxons, Runes, and Magic," in *Journal of the Archeological Association*, 1964, pp. 14–31.

12 *Runes and Germanic Linguistics*, op. cit., p. 39. See also Elmer H. Antonsen, "On the Mythological Interpretation of the Oldest Runic Inscriptions," in Mohammad Ali Jazayery and Werner Winter (ed.), *Languages and Cultures. Studies in Honor of Edgar C. Polomé*, Mouton-de Gruyter, Berlin 1988, pp. 43–54.

On the contrary, Gerd Høst is one of those who think that taking into account magic is crucial to grasp the history of the runes. He reckons that "magic-writing (*skriftmagien*) is older than the fully-fledged writing system. Its roots must go as far back as the prehistory of writing, symbolic and religious magic, the pictorial world of rupestrian inscriptions and symbols of protection and destruction of all kinds."[13] Likewise, according to Ralph W. V. Elliott, "the runes were never solely utilitarian: since they were picked up by the Germanic people, they were used for divination and other rites. Throughout runic writing's long history, interpersonal communication took a back seat to invoking higher powers in order to affect the lives and the fate of men."[14] Therefore Elliot thinks that the runes were first used for "magical" purposes before being used as a writing, and he thinks that as symbols, their origins are

> the pre-runic pictures and the pictorial symbols engraved on the rocks and stones of ancient Germanic lands, lands where the runes were profoundly associated with the religious beliefs and ritual practices of the pagan and Germanic Antiquity.[15]

René L. M. Derolez writes in the same vein that

> the runes have been manifestly used for religious and magical purposes for a long time. The signs used to hold a secret power that exceeded the literal meaning of the inscriptions.[16]

In that conversation which seems to never end,[17] some runologists adopted a middle of the road perspective. While pointing out that "the obsession

---

13 Gerd Høst, *Runer. Våre eldste norske runeinskrifter*, W. Aschehoug & Co., Oslo 1976, p. 15.
14 *Runes. An Introduction*, op. cit., pp. 1–2 (see p. 42 above).
15 Ibid.
16 *Les dieux et la religion des Germains*, op. cit., p. 27.
17 Stephen Flowers, whose views can be questionable, offered a good summary on the question: *Runes and Magic. Magical Formulaic Elements in the Older Runic Tradition*, Peter Lang, New York 1986. On the same topic, see also Karl Martin Nielsen, "Runen und Magie. Ein forschungsgeschichtlicher Überblick," in *Frühmittelalterliche Studien*, 1985, pp. 75–97; Peter Buchholz, "Die Runen in religion und Magie. Eddische Zeugnisse zu den Runen — runische Zeugnisse zur vorchristlichen nordgermanischen Religion," in Etudes germaniques, October-December 1997, pp. 563–580; Robert Nedoma, "Zur Problematik der Deutung älterer Runeninschriften — kultisch, magisch oder profan?,"

some runologists have with magic has more to do with the psychology of scholars than with the inherent content of the inscriptions they study,"[18] Lucien Musset underlines that the runes could very well have had magical uses as well as secular ones:

> The runes are not magical, they only were sometimes used for magic [...] As far as their magical inclination is real, it seems to have been reliant on the minority that knew how to trace and interpret them, it was not inherent to their nature.[19]

It's quite obvious that the runes were first used for secular and magical/religious purposes, but that doesn't tell us why there are so many "magical" texts among the first inscriptions, which can't quite be explained by saying that "a minority knew how to trace and interpret them." For that matter, Musset even notes that

> it is because of their magical use, whether actual or assumed, that the last users of the *Fuþark* were sometimes struck with ecclesiastic excommunication since. It occurred since at least the end of the 16th century and predominantly in Iceland."[20]

Likewise, when Alain Marez writes that "there is agreement that runic signs aren't inherently magical, but that there were sometimes used for magical purposes,"[21] he begs the question, because we could just as well argue that the signs lost their original magical property and that it was lost progressively as they became used for writing. But, of course, we need to distinguish

---

in Klaus Düwel and Sean Nowak (Hg.), *Runeninschriften als Quellen interdisziplinärer Forschung*, op. cit., pp. 24–55; John McKinnell, Rudolf Simek and Klaus Düwel, *Runes, Magic and Religion. A Sourcebook*, Fassbaender, Wien 2004; Mindy MacLeod and Bernard Mees, *Runic Amulets and Magic Objects*, Boydell Press, Woodbridge 2006. See also the pages Georges Dumézil wrote on Norse magic in *La saga de Hadingus (Saxo Grammaticus I, V-VIII). Du mythe au roman*, PUF, Paris 1953, as well as René L. M. Derolez, "La divination chez les Germains," in André Caquot and Marcel Leibovici (ed.), La divination, vol. 1, PUF, Paris 1968, pp. 257–302.

18 *Introduction à la runologie*, op. cit., pp. 142 and 155.

19 Ibid., p. 145.

20 Ibid., p. 141.

21 *Anthologie runique*, op. cit., p. 85.

between using the runes to trace a "magical" inscription and holding them to be inherently "magical" characters.

Even if Régis Boyer is very hostile to those "who are convinced of the religious or magical uses and nature or value of the writing of the ancient Germanic people,"[22] he acknowledges that "the texts our knowledge of the North's religion is derived from are literally drenched in magic [...] It feels necessary to someone who wants to understand to assume at all times a backdrop made of a whole bunch of magical practices and words, conceptions related to sorcery," which makes him suspect that the runes were originally used "mostly for magical words, and they were certainly associated with supernatural powers."[23]

Lucien Musset admits that it seems impossible to exclude magic from five large groups of texts:

> Those which contain the same rune repeated several times without any rational meaning for it [...] those which contain some incomprehensible or unpronounceable sentences when they have been positively deciphered [...] those which were placed in tombs so that they weren't accessible to people from this world and also contain unintelligible sentences or conjurations [...] those which clearly contain curses or spells [...] those whose author call himself a 'priest,' a 'magician,' or anything like it [...] and finally those which contain one of the 'keywords' of Nordic magic: *alu*, *laukaR* and maybe *laþu-*. Those three mysterious terms are relatively frequent in ancient texts.[24]

The magical character of many inscriptions in the Old *Fuþark* can actually hardly be contested. Yes, not all ancient inscriptions are "magical," but the ones that are linked to magic are so plentiful that it can not be fortuitous. How could this be if the magical character or power of the runes were only a secondary or late derived belief? Musset quite correctly makes a reference to some undecipherable or hardly comprehensible inscriptions, like the ones that only repeat the same rune or sequence of runes (*gagaga* on the lance-shaft of Kragehul, which associates the runes **gebō* and **ansuz*, *aaaaaaaa* on the amulet of Lindholmen, etc.). If some of those runic inscriptions can't be

---

22 *Etudes germaniques*, October–December 1997, p. 510.

23 Régis Boyer, *L'Edda poétique*, Fayard, Paris 1992, p. 619. See also Régis Boyer, Le monde du double. *La magie chez les anciens Scandinaves*, Paris 1986.

24 *Introduction à la runologie*, op. cit., pp. 146–150.

deciphered, it should be because they hadn't transcribed words yet, rather than they looked like letters the engraver used according to their original magical meaning.

After a careful examination of the arguments for and against it, Klaus Düwel and Wilhelm Heizmann sided with a magical interpretation of a large number of the most ancient runic inscriptions.[25] "One cannot separate the use of the runes from practicing magic" also writes Alain Marez, and then he adds:

> That tight connection which goes through various degrees of the epigraphic tradition from its origins to its disappearance is apparent in the simple fact that [runic] signs are sometimes not meant to transcribe a linguistic fact like the notation of an oral excerpt, but rather it transcribes an extra-linguistic value of the sign, meaning a mental representation it implies thanks to the acrophonic principle.[26]

---

25 Klaus Düwel and Wilhelm Heizmann, "Das ältere Fuþark—Überlieferung und Wirkungsmöglichkeiten der Runenreihe," in Alfred Bammesberger and Gaby Waxenberger (ed.), *Reallexikon der Germanischen Altertumskunde*, vol. 51, op. cit., p. 45. See also Klaus Düwel, "Runen als magischen Zeichen," in Peter Ganz and Malcom Parkes (ed.), *Das Buch als magisches und als Repräsentationsobjekt*, Otto Harrassowitz, Wiesbaden 1992, pp. 87–100; "Magische Runenzeichen und magische Runeninschriften," in Staffan Nyström (ed.), Runor och ABC. *Elva föreläsningar från ett symposium i Stockholm våren 1995*, Stockholms Medeltidsmuseum Stockholm 1997, pp. 23–41.

26 *Anthologie runique*, op. cit., p. 158.

16

The Word "Rune"

THE MODERN USE OF the word "rune" (Danish *rune*, Swedish *runa*) was borrowed from the Scandinavian languages in the 17th century, but the term refers to the *Fuþark's* letters since at least the 4th century. Confirmed in the 6th century as *runa*, the term seems to have been mentioned for the time as *rūnō* (plural *rūnōR*) in the inscription of the Einang stone from Norway, which goes back to the second half of the 4th century: *dagaR þaR rūnō faihidō*, "(I) Dagr I colored the runes."[1] We find it again in the funereal inscription of the Järsberg stone, found in 1862 in the Swedish province of Värmland, which dates from around 530: ...*runoRw aritu* "I engraved the runes."

Some authors tried to link the *run-* root (which is derived from Proto-Germanic **runō-*) back to the ancient Indo-European stem **wr-th-enā*. Georges Dumézil also linked the names of the Greek and Indian gods Ouranos and Váruna to it ("binding" gods, if one decides to make those names be derived from the root **wer-* "binding," but also whose name can mean "oath" or "true words" if one decides to make them be derived from the root **wer-* "speaking").[2] But that is very disputable. The root **rew-* "shouting" (see Latin *rumor*) doesn't work either.

---

[1] The expression "to color the runes" is often encountered in inscriptions as well as in the Poetic Edda. It really seems like the runes were originally painted in red or colored with blood. See François-Xavier Dillmann, "Les runes dans la littérature norroise," in *Proxima Thulé*, 2, 1996, pp. 66–67.

[2] Georges Dumézil, *Mythes et dieux des Germains*, PUF, Paris 1939, p. 24.

The consistent meaning of the term is whisper, secret, mystery, hidden thing, which seems to confirm that the runes were first used for magical purposes or meant for the few In Old High German, *rūna* "secret, secret conversation," *rún* in Old Norse "secret, mysterious conference," *rūna* in Old Saxon "secret, mystery," *rūna* in Gothic "mystery," *rūn* in Old English "secret, consultation, whisper," and the plural *rūnar* in Icelandic "secrets, mysterious conferences" are a testament to it. The same meaning can be found in Celtic languages with *rún* in Old Irish "secret, mystery, ulterior motive," *rhin* in Welsh "secret, mystery," *rhin* in Middle Welsh "secret, mystery," *rùn* in Gaelic "secret, ulterior motive," *rhin* in Welsh "secret property, mystery," and *run* in Irish "secret." See also *runo* in Finnish "charm, ancient song, epic or magic song."[3] Besides those nominal forms, there are also verbal forms: *rūnen* in Old High German "whispering, speaking quietly," *rūnian* in Old English "murmuring, whispering," *rýna* in Old Norse "talking intimately," *runian* in Old English "speaking softly," *reonian* in Old Anglo-Saxon "murmuring," *rýna* in Icelandic "having a secret conversation" *to round* in English, etc. The Gothic translation of the Bible still uses the word *runa* to translate "mystery" (*runa thiudangardos Gudis* "mysteries of the kingdom of God," Mark 4.11). In *Beowulf* (8th century), the royal councillor is called *Run-Wita*, "versed in secrets." All those words give us reason to believe that the runes were originally believed to have some secret aspect.[4]

The alternative etymology of the word "rune" suggested by Erik Moltke (who argues that the "mystery" or "secret" meanings are secondary) that uses the root *ru* "making a sound, making some noise" and that was supposedly originally used as an onomatopoeia, absolutely not convincing since runes are writing signs and therefore obviously don't make any sound (they enable writing, not talking). Other authors tried to derive the name of the runes from an Indo-European root that means "scratching"[5] or tried to give them the simple meaning of "inscription, message" (Elmer H. Antonsen). Those suggestions clearly seem to be gratuitous.

---

3   See Wolfgang Krause, "Zur Herkunft von finn. runo 'Lied'," in Finnischugrischen *Forschungen*, 1969, pp. 91–97.

4   See Terence W. Wilbur, "The Word 'Rune'," in *Scandinavian Studies*, 1957, pp. 12–18.

5   Richard L. Morris, "Northwest-Germanic *rūn-* 'rune': A Case of Homonymy with Go. *rūna* 'mystery'," in *Beiträge zur Geschichte der deutschen Sprache und Literatur*, 1985, pp. 344–358.

The name of the runes can also be found in female names such as Gudrun, Sigrun, Heidrun, Waldrun, Runhilde, etc., as well as in the denomination of the mandrake's root, *Alraun* (see *Alrūna* in Tacitus's *Germania*, 8). The mandrake is a hardy herbaceous plant that has been associated with magical beliefs and rituals since Antiquity, perhaps because it is vaguely human-shaped and because of its hallucinogenic properties. It is interesting to note that in the Middle Ages, the plant was believed to predominantly grow at the bottom of gallows, because it was said to be impregnated with the sperm of the hanged men (whose god was Óðinn). It was also used in ointments that were said to be made by "witches." In the history of the Goths written in 551 by the Latin-speaking historian Jordanes, there is a passage on the king Filimer that alludes to witches: "*magas mulieres quas patrio sermone haliurrunnas is ipse cognominat*," "Female witches that were called in the national language *haliurrunnas*" (*Getica*, XXIV, 121). That word *haliurrunnas* was interpreted by Karl Müllenhoff as referring to the Gothic form **haljō-rūnas*, like *helrūn*, *helrūne* or *hellerūne* in Old English "witch, female magician" or *helerūna* or *helliruna* in Old High German "sorcery, necromancy." Like other female proper nouns with *-rūn*, it is compound possessive: "the [female] ones who know the infernal secret." The first term **haljō* is a plural genitive of *halja* in Gothic "inferno, underworld, shadow world" (see *hell* in English, *Hölle* in German). It seems that witches or female magicians were regarded as the holders of the runes' secret.[6]

---

6   In the *Gesta Danorum* (I, VI, 4–5), this is the case of Harthgrepa, who is presented by Saxo Grammaticus as a woman who engages in necromancian rites with the help of runic signs. Georges Dumézil translated and commented on that passage in *La Saga de Hadingus*, op. cit., pp. 76–82.

17

Divination and Oracular Use

It seems to us that René L. M. Derolez paints the picture perfectly when he writes that the partition into three *ættir* "is probably linked to the custom of casting spells three times in a row." He adds:

> When spells were cast, the characters were read by announcing their names. Each name corresponded to a short verse which explained its meaning. The rune *n*, which was called 'misery,' 'misfortune,' 'violence,' likely heralded misfortune, whereas *g*, 'gift,' 'wealth,' 'favor,' or *j*, 'good year,' 'bountiful harvest,' heralded the favor of the gods. The order of the signs in the runic alphabet differs from the orders of other alphabets, the reason for this should be found in its divinatory use.[1]

Wherever runes were used, including Iceland and Greenland, there are good reasons to believe that they were used for magical or divinatory purposes. François-Xavier Dillmann speaks of "the old Scandinavian custom of engraving mysterious signs or runes in the middle of magico-religious sessions."[2] As a result of that tradition of consulting fate and observing auspices, the Church multiplied its condemnations in the Middle Ages.

A crucial testimony on that topic is in our possession. The Roman historian Tacitus writes about the Germanic people in *Germania* in 98 that:

> They value auspices and fate more than anybody else, their method to know those is quite simple: they cut a branch from a fruit tree and chop it up into

---

1   *Les dieux et la religion des Germains*, op. cit., pp. 173–174.
2   *Les magiciens dans l'Islande ancienne*, op. cit., p. 125.

small logs, then, after marking them with distinctive signs, they randomly throw them onto a piece of white cloth. Then a priest of the tribe if the consultation is official or the head of the household if the consultation is private invokes the gods and, while watching the skies, he picks up three logs to interpret based on the signs engraved in them.³

The crux of the matter is within those few lines which demonstrate that Germanic people used some signs for oracular purposes. To know their fate, the officiant randomly picks three engraved logs and gathers them for interpretation. Just like *légein* in Greek or *legere* in Latin "to say," *lesen* in German first meant "to gather, to assemble, to choose," a meaning that's still present in *lesan* in Anglo-Saxon, *lesa* in Norse, and *galisan* in Gothic. The phrase "while watching the skies" should also be underlined. Unfortunately, Tacitus doesn't mention how many logs there were and whether the number was always the same. He mentions "signs" (*notæ*) and not letters (*literæ*), and he doesn't elaborate on their nature or form either.

It is also tough to say which signs he was talking about beside runes and runic symbols (*Begriffsrunen*), especially since we now know that Tacitus' description is contemporary to all the first known runic inscriptions.⁴

---

3   Tacitus, *La Germanie. L'origine et le pays des Germains*, chap. 10, Arléa, Paris 2009, pp. 36–37, translation Patrick Voisin. Original text: "*Auspiciam sortesque ut qui maxime observant: sortium consuetudo simplex: virgam frugiferas arbori decisam in surculos amputant eosque notis quibusdam discretos super candidam vestem temere ac fortuito spargunt. Mox, si publice consultatur, sacerdos civitatis, sin privatim, ipse pater familiæ, precatus deos cælumque suspiciens, ter singulos tollit, sublatos secundum impressam ante notam interpretatur.*" There is also a translation by Pierre Grimal: "Les mœurs des Germains," in Tacitus, *Œuvres choisies*, Club du meilleur livre, Paris 1959, pp. 33–48. Grimal uses the terms "stick" (and not "branch"), "pieces" (and not "some logs") and "different signs." Tacitus, born around 56, died around 117. The exact title of his book should be *De origine et situ Germanorum*, a title mentioned in the *Hersfeldensis*, inventory of the monastery of Hersfeld, delivered in 1451 to the pontifical legate Enoch of Escoli so that he could hand it to the Roman Curia, like the pope Nicolas V wanted. We know *Germania* from that version, which was published for the first time in 1473 in Nuremberg, Germany. Since it was published before the 15th century, some authors wondered whether the text we have in our possession is true copy of the original. See the Eugen Fehrle's presentation of the Latin-German bilingual edition published in 1957 by Winker in Heidelberg.

4   In another passage of his book, Tacitus writes that men and women of Germania don't write to each other: "When it comes to letters and their secrets, both men and women are ignorant" (*literarum secreta viri pariter ac feminæ ignorant*), according to Patrick Voisin's translation (op. cit., p. 48). But Pierre Grimal prefers the following: "Men and

Many runologists acknowledge this, like Georg Baesecke, Arthur Mentz,[5] Wolfgang Krause, Helmut Arntz, Karl Schneider, Ralph W. V. Elliott,[6] Elmar Seebold,[7] etc. "Tacitus clearly states that three signs were picked to be interpreted and many suggest that that number corresponds to the three *ættir*," writes Bernard Mees, who thinks "it hard to see how Tacitus could point to something else than the runes."[8] "It is not absurd to assume that the oracular process could have had two roles in the formation of the *Fuþark* once it was picked up by the Germanic people," writes Lucien Musset: "it could have influenced the order of the signs and it could have helped to choose the names of the signs since they seem so fitting, like **fehu* 'wealth,' **wunjō* 'joy,' or **nauþiz* 'distress,' maybe because the runes looked like the *notæ* that had the same meaning and were used before them."[9]

Tacitus didn't go to Germania but he adapted the descriptions he could get his hands on. Pliny the Elder (23–79) probably knew the Germanic people better than him since he had served as a Roman officer in the Rhine region. Unfortunately, his book *Germaniæ libri XX* was lost, but it is likely that Tacitus had access to it when he wrote his book. The information Tacitus gives should also be compared with what is written about the ancient Germanic people by authors like Plutarch, Strabo, Suetonius, Livy or Ammianus Marcellinus. The divinatory process he talks of corresponds perfectly to what the Greek historian Herodotus wrote about the Scythians and the Alani. The random picking was also done by the Cimbri and the

---

women equally ignore clandestine correspondence" ("Les mœurs des Germains," p. 43), a sentence with a very different meaning. Tacitus doesn't mean that Germanic people don't know how to write, but rather that they don't form adulterous relationships with the help of secret love letters, unlike in Rome (he explains that "there is very little adultery in such a large nation").

5   Arthur Mentz, "Die 'notæ' der Germanen bei Tacitus," in *Rheinisches Museum für Philologie*, 1937, pp. 193–205.

6   *Runes. An Introduction*, op. cit., p. 66.

7   "Was haben die Germanen mit den Runen gemacht?," art. cit.

8   "Runes in the First Century," art. cit., pp. 221–222. See also Allan A. Lund, "Zum Germanenbegriff bei Tacitus," in Heinrich Beck (Hg.), *Germanenprobleme in heutiger Sicht*, op. cit., pp. 53–87; "Zur Gesamtinterpretation der 'Germania' des Tacitus," in Hildegard Temporini and Wolfgang Haase (ed.), *Aufstieg und Niedergang der römischen Welt. Geschichte und Kultur Roms im Spiegel der neueren Forschung. II. Principat. 33. Sprache und Literatur*, 3, Walter de Gruyter, Berlin 1991, pp. 1858–1988.

9   *Introduction à la runologie*, op. cit., p. 155.

Suebi (Plutarch, *Marius*, 15, 4). Caesar reported that fate was consulted three times to decide what should happen to Valerius Procillus and Willibrod, two Romans that were captured by Germans, and every time the gods chose to let them live (*De bello gallico*, I, 53). Such tales are comparable to the *Song of Hymir* (*Hymiskvida*), collected in the Poetic Edda, where it reads: "Long ago the warlike divinities, / assemble to feast [...] / threw their magical sticks / and examined the victim's fate" (str. 1).

Consulting fate by using some signs engraved on pieces of wood seems also to have been done by the Italic people. In *De divinatione* (II, 85), Cicero evokes the different ways to consult fate, notably the oracles of Praeneste (*sortes Prænestinæ*). He writes:

> The annals of Praeneste tell us that Numerius Suffustius, a respectable man from a noble family, dreamt several times that he was ordered in an increasingly threatening fashion to go to a specific location to carve rocks. Afraid, he obeyed despite the mocking from his fellow citizens and from the broken rocks came down pieces of oak-tree wood bearing antique characters (*itaque perfracto saxo sortis erupisse in robore insculptas priscarum litterarum notis*). That location is surrounded by an enclosure nowadays and dedicated to child Jupiter that can be seen there with Juno.

Later in the book, Cicero mentions again fate is consulted from "pieces of olive-tree wood." He adds: "who brought the oak down, carved it and engraved characters?" That illusion is not negligible, especially since Cicero is talking about *litterarœ notœ* "written characters, letters," and that sheds light on why Tacitus used the same word as well.[10]

---

10 There is a curious passage in the *Iliad* where Homer writes that Prœtus, king of Argos, sent Bellerophon to Lycia to meet its king who is his stepfather, "and delivered to him a gruesome message, sealed tablets that bore death signs" (VI, 168, translation Ch. Georgin and W. Berthaut). In Paul Mazon's translation, the same passage reads: "He sent Bellerophon to Lycia while giving to him gruesome signs. He had traced many deadly signs on folded tablets." The text indicates that the king of Lycia welcomed his guest "for nine days" and "had nine steers killed for him" (VI, 170). Maybe we should bring up that the Chinese *Yijing* ("Book of mutations") is made trigrams, which are sequences of eight symbols made of segments of straight lines laid out on three levels (8 x 3, like in the ættir). Chinese tradition tells us that the Emperor Fu Xi who reigned in the 18th century BC was the one who created it. Chinese ideographic writing was created around the end of the Shang dynasty, in the 13th or 12th century BC. The first inscriptions (*buci*), which were inscribed in bovid bones and turtle breastplates had essentially oraculary or divinatory characteristics, which gives us

In the 8th century, the *Lex Frisionum* still mentions the Germanic habit to consult fate by throwing "signs." "Quæ sorte tales esse debent: duo tali de virga præcisi, quos tenos vocant, quorum unus signo crusis innotatur, alius purus dimittitur, et lana munda obvoluti super altare seu reliquias mittuntur" (XIII, 1). In Middle High German, *zeichen* ("sign"), which is derived from Old High German *zeihhan*, incidentally means "omen" (just like in Latin). In Charlemagne's time, the Carolingian monk Hrabanus Maurus (776–859) who was the abbot of Fulda and archbishop of Mainz, evokes in his *De inventione litterarum* that the Marcomanni used "letters" (*literas*) for the purposes of divinatory invocations (*cum quibus [literas] carmina sua incantationesque ac divinationes significare procurant, qui adhuc pagano ritu involvuntur*). Another version uses the word *runstabas* instead of *literas*, but it could be a later text that was put under Hrabanus Maurus' patronage in retrospect to give it more authority. In the 9th century, Rimbert's *Vita Ansgari* also mentions the "random pick." Saxo Grammaticus (1150–1216) evokes in his history of Denmark (Gesta Danorum) about Hamlet (Amleth) "letters inscribed in wooden tables" (*literas ligno insculptas*). In the 11th century, the abbot Ælfric associates the runes with magic in one of his homilies: "thurh drýcræft oththe thurh rúnstafum," "by magic or by the runes."[11]

---

reason to believe that those were the functions of the first ideograms. We still don't know whether that first Chinese writing was actually autochthonous. See Kwang-chih Chang, *Shang Civilization*, Yale University Press, New Haven 1980; Jean-Pierre Voiret, "Runenalphabet(e) im Vor-antiken China?," in *Asiatische Studien — Etudes asiatiques*, 1997, 4, pp. 1047–1053.

11 See Ralph W. V. Elliott, Runes. *An Introduction*, op. cit., p. 69.

18

"Magic" Vocabulary

DESPITE ANDERS BÆKSTED'S OPINION,[1] it seems to me that like Lucien Musset pointed out, some runic inscriptions in Old *Fuþark* were originally put in tombs. The fact that these mortuary deposits were out of people's sight makes a case for them having a magico-religious character. That is the case of the Kylver stone's inscription, which was part of the sepulcher's funeral offerings, and beside a complete *Fuþark*, it also includes magical signs (*seus*), which more likely than not is meant to convey a spell. "The inscription is not meant to be read directly by the living, because aside the fact that it was put inside a tomb, it faces towards the earth," underlines Alain Marez.[2] It is also the case of the Noleby Runestone (Sweden, 6th century) found in 1894 in Västergötland, which has two graphic sequences that have not been deciphered, and the Eggja stone (Norway, 8th century), which was part of a tomb that was partially destroyed. The Eggja stone has the longest known inscription in Old *Fuþark* (120 runes long, forbidding people from unveiling the stone).

Some words present in runic inscriptions belong to the magic vocabulary on their own: *auja, alu, laþu (laðu), laukaR, ota, eh(þ)u*, etc. The meaning of the word *alu*, which can be found more than twenty times in inscriptions,

---

[1] Anders Bæksted, "Begravede runestene," in *Aarbøger for nordisk oldkyndighed og historie*, 1951 [1952], pp. 63–95.

[2] *Anthologie runique*, op. cit., p. 99. See also Sven B. F. Jansson, *Runes in Sweden*, Royal Academy of Letters, History and Antiquities, Stockholm 1987, p. 13.

in particular on the Elgesem runestone (Norway, 5th century), the amulets of Kinneved (Sweden, around 600) and Lindholmen (Sweden, 5th century), and the ring of Körlin (Poland, 6th century), remains unsettled. Some, like Sophus Bugge, link it to *ealgian* "to protect" in Old English and claim it means "defense, protection." For phonological reasons, Gerd Høst prefers linking it to the name of the beer used for libations (Old Norse *ol*), especially since the *olrunar* were inscribed *á horni* "on a [drinking] horn." Edgar C. Polomé, who shares this opinion, links the term to *alýein* "being outside one's self" in Greek and to *alwanzatar-* "magic, witchcraft" in Hittite to claim that it means "ecstasy," which leads him to wonder whether "beer got its name from its primordial function in magico-religious purposes?"[3]

The Proto-Nordic term *erilaR* or *ek erilaR* ("me, the *erilaR*") that can be found in some runic inscriptions was also a hot topic of debate. It can notably be on the amulet of Lindholmen — *ek erilaR sāwīlagaR ha(i)teka* — the Väsby bracteate, the Bratsberg fibula, the Järsberg Runestone, the Kragehul spear shaft, etc. Sophus Bugge believed it was the name of a runesmith that was part of the Heruli tribe (**erulāz*), which was also the opinion of Wolfgang Krause and Helmut Arntz. Jacobsen and Moltke simply take it as the ethnic name of the Herules (*eruli* or *Heruli* in Latin, *érouloi* in Greek), a people we know little about beside that they more likely did not come from Denmark and were expelled by the Danes. From the 3rd to the 5th century, they spread across various region of Europe, from Gaul to Moravia and near the Black Sea.[4] However, according to Otto Höfler, the Heruli were not exactly a people, but rather some kind of cultic aristocracy related to warlike mentoring (*Kriegerverband*) and involved Germanic people from several tribes, whose use of runes was both cryptic and religious.[5] A member of that band of "Odinian" warriors allegedly served as an auxiliary in the Roman

---

3   Edgar C. Polomé, "Notes sur le vocabulaire religieux du germanique I: Runique alu," in *La Nouvelle Clio*, 1954, p. 55. See also Edgar C. Polomé, "Beer, Runes and Magic," in *The Journal of Indo-European Studies*, 1996, pp. 99–105; Gerd Høst, "Trylleordet alu," in *Norske Vitenskaps-Akademi Årbok*, 1980, pp. 35–49; Ute Zimmermann, "Bier, Runen und Macht: Ein Formelwort im Kontext," in *Futhark. International Journal of Runic Studies*, V, 2014, pp. 45–64.

4   See Palle Lauring, *The Land of the Tollund Man*, Lutterworth Press, London 1957, pp. 142–143, which made of the Heruli the creators of the *Fuþark*.

5   Otto Höfler, "Herkunft und Ausbreitung des Runen," in *Die Sprache*, 1971, pp. 134–156.

army and created runic writing from north Italic alphabets from the Alps. The term *erilaR* or *irilaR* then supposedly referred to a person versed in the ways to read and inscribe runes.⁶ Höfler mainly relied on the inscription *C(enturia) Erul(i)* on the Negau A helmet for his theory, which still continues to be widely discussed.⁷

That term has finally been linked to the more recent Old Norse title of *jarl* "high rank chief, duke, count," which refers to someone with a high social status, but it raises phonological concerns. It should be noted that in the Poetic Edda, the *Rígsþula* poem narrates the formation of the social hierarchy in ancient Scandinavia. It says that Rígr (Heimdall) taught rune-smithing to one of his three sons, Jarl, forebear of the noble class (str. 33–36).⁸ According to Anders Hultgård, the expression *ek erilaR* could be interpreted as theophany formula, which implies a situation where a divinity manifests itself to a man or a group of men.⁹

---

6   Olof Sundqvist simply speaks of a "*ritual specialist*" ("Contributions of the Oldest Runic Inscriptions to the Reconstruction of Ancient Scandinavian Religion. Some Methodological Reflections with Reference to an Example of the Phenomenological Category of 'Ritual Specialists'"), in Oliver Grimm and Alexandra Pesch, Hg., *Archäologie und Runen. Fallstudien zu Inschriften im älteren Futhark*, op. cit., pp. 121–143).

7   See Robert Nedoma, *Die Inschrift auf dem Helm B von Negau. Möglichkeiten und Grenzen der Deutung norditalischer epigraphischer Denkmäler*, Fassbaender, Wien 1995 (against Höfler, pp. 18–19).

8   Jarl supposedly refers to **erlāz* in common Germanic, and not **erilāz* in common Germanic. See Harry Andersen, "Om urnordisk erilaR og jarl," in *Sprog og Kultur*, 1948, pp. 97–102. On the difficulties involved in derivating jarl *erilaR*, see also Eric Elgqvist, *Studier rörande Njordkultens spridning bland de nordiska folken*, Olin, Lund 1952, pp. 117–135; Bernard Mees, "Runic erilaR," in *Nowele*, 2003, pp. 41–68. On the *Rígsþula*, see Georges Dumézil, "La Rígsþula et la structure sociale indo-européenne," in *Revue de l'histoire des religions*, 1958, pp. 1–9; François-Xavier Dillmann, "La Rígsþula. Traduction française du poème eddique," in *Proxima Thulé*, 5, 2006, pp. 59–72; "La Rígsþula. Présentation d'ensemble du poème eddique et état de la recherché," in Vittoria Dolcetti Corazza and Renato Gendre (ed.), *Lettura dell'Edda. Poesia e prosa*, Edizioni dell'Orso, Alessandria 2006, pp. 85–114.

9   Ander Hultgård, "Formules de théophanie, de la Scandinavie à l'Iran," in *Comptes rendus de l'Académie des Inscriptions et Belles-lettres*, 6 February 2009, pp. 205–240. The author make a suggested link between various Theophanic formulas attested in Indo-Iranian domains and Vedic domains, which originally were recited during public worship.

19

Óðinn and the "Divine Origin" of the Runes

"THERE IS ONE AND ONLY ONE THING Nordic tradition is unanimous about: the runes are God-made. A human inventor is never mentioned," writes Lucien Musset.[1] There are indeed multiple inscriptions that describe the runes as "birthed by the gods" or "came from the gods" (*reginkunnar*). The Noleby runestone reads *Rūnō fahi raginakudo* "I paint the runes that come from the gods," and the Sparlösa runestone (Sweden, early 11th century) reads *runaR þaR ræginkundu* "those runes that come out of the gods." The runes are also described as *reginkunnr* (of divine origin) in the Edda (*Hávamál*, str. 80) which indicates that they were created by the *ginregin*, "almighty gods" (str. 142).[2] The Old Norse word *regin* is a collective designation for the gods, which means in the proper sense "decisions, sentences," a bit like *numina deorum*. The appellative *ginregin* adds to the neutral plural *regin* the reinforcing prefix *gin-* that can be found in the name of the original abyss of Scandinavian cosmology, the *Ginnungagap*.

---

1 *Introduction à la runologie*, op. cit., p. 168.
2 The compound *reginkunnr*, "of divine origin," also meant of "divine nature." See Maurice Cahen, "L'adjectif 'divin' en germanique," in *Mélanges offerts à M. Charles Andler par ses amis et ses élèves*, Strasbourg 1924, pp. 79–107; François-Xavier Dillmann, "Les runes dans la littérature norroise," art. cit., pp. 77–78. See also Mario Polia, *Le rune e gli dèi del Nord*, Il Cerchio, Rimini 1999.

But the "divine" character of the runes is above all else related to their discovery by the god Óðinn, as narrated by the Poetic Edda in one of the most famous passages of that great poem named the *Hávamál* (the "tales of the Most-High" = Óðinn). The text dates from the 12th or the 13th century, but most of of the work, which is split into verses, was most likely written before 950, from much older traditions and using much older materials, since the first and older part of the *Hávamál* is already quoted by the skald Eyvindr Skáldaspillir in 980.[3] The verses 138–145, which form the fifth part of the poem, are called *Rúnatal* (*Rúnaþáttr Óðinns*), meaning the (count of the runes.) This is Óðinn speaking:

> For nights all nine,
> I know that I hung
> on that wyrd and windy tree,
> by gar wounded
> and given to Odin,
> myself to myself I gave,
> on that mammoth tree
> of which Man knows not
> from where the roots do run.
>
> Blessed with no bread,
> nor brimming horn,
> down below I looked;
> Runes I took up,
> roaring I took them,
> then back unbound I fell.
>
> With mighty songs nine
> from that much-famed son
> of Bestla's father Bolthorn,
> a draft I drank
> of the dearest mead,
> from the Stirrer of Poetry poured.

---

3   "The Poetic Edda," writes Régis Boyer, "indisputably goes back to an oral tradition that the scribes of the 13th century didn't really understand anymore, like the errors they often made in their transcriptions show […] Those poems were obviously spread from word of mouth for centuries before they were written down." (*L'Edda* poétique, op. cit., p. 73). The Poetic Edda has been rediscovered in 1643 by the Icelandic bishop Brynjulf Sveinsson (1605–1675).

Then fertile I became
and full of wisdom,
and I grew and greatly thrived.
A word got a word
by a word for me;
a work got a work
by a work for me.

Runes you will find
and readable staves,
very strong those staves,
very stiff those staves,
which were painted by the mighty priest,
and rendered by the high rulers,
and risted by the rulers' invoker.[4]

So, it is in that famous text that Scandinavian tradition attributes the discovery of the runes to Óðinn. It should be emphasized that it's a discovery, not an invention, because the text implies that the runes existed prior to the story being told. Every word must be carefully considered. It is after having hanged for "nine full nights" (*netr allar nío*) from a "windy" tree and having looked down ("down below"), that the god could "take up the runes" (*nysta ek niþr, nam ek upp rúnar*). Then he learned from the giant Bölthorn nine "mighty songs" (*fimbulljódh níu*), meaning nine magical songs filled with energy, which enabled him to "become fertile," to "become full of wisdom," to "grow," and to "thrive." The "windy" tree is Yggdrasil (Yggr's horse), the world tree, the cosmic tree of the ancient Germanic people. Sometimes described as a yew tree (*Eibe* in German), sometimes as an ash tree, it protects the world it supports and it is the main residence of the gods. It could correspond to the rune thirteen (ᛇ), which is called *ῑwaz* "yew" (*īwa* in Old High German, *īo* in Anglo-Saxon, *ibe* in Danish, *jubhar* in Irish, etc.). The "very strong staves" or "very stiff staves" could have been used for divination or magic. We should note the allusions to the "high rulers" and "rulers' invoker" (*hroptr rögna, Hroptatýr*), which is one of the aliases of Óðinn.

---

4   Ibid., pp. 196–197, translation Régis Boyer.

That initiatory hanging which enabled Óðinn to discover the runes has often been used as a pretext to attribute "shamanic" traits to him, and we should exercise caution when it comes to that interpretation because "shamanism" explanations have been overused, and that term should be handled more carefully than it usually is. Fraçoise Bader rightly underlined the *visual* character of that acquisition, by reminding us that the same Indo-European root **weyd-* expresses both notions of "seeing" and "knowing."[5] Óðinn, who left one of his eyes in the Mímir's well does indeed have a great "vision."

Like Varuna for the Indians or Ogmios for the Celts, Óðinn embodies night sky, the dark aspect of cosmic sovereignty (in opposition to Týr), and he patronizes magic in this respect. He can also be compared to Ouranos for the Greeks or Jupiter Stator for the Romans. "Óðinn is a runesmith," writes Bernard Sergent, "because he is an extension of the kind of gods who master magic."[6] Sovereign magician, "binding" god, but also "shouting" god, like Indra for the Indo-Aryans he has the power of metamorphosis. God of war, patron of "bestial warriors" (*Berserkir*), father of the dead, master of the wild hunt, he is also the god of drunkenness and ecstasy.

Óðinn is called Othinn in Old Swedish, Wōden in Anglo-Saxon, Wodan in Old Saxon, Wotan or Wuotan in Old High German. All those forms are derived from the primitive form **Wōdan(az)* or **Wōdinaz*, which is probably also related to *vates* (*uātēs*) in Latin and *ouateis* in Celtic. The etymology of the term take it back to *ód* "fury" (Old Norse *óðr*), hence *Wut* in German (from Old High German *wuot*) and *woede* in Dutch, same meaning. The fury in question is both a fighting fury and a "spiritual elation that is almost ecstatic," which can be expressed by a "visionary vaticination" (Edgar C. Polomé). Adam of Bremen writes: "*Wodan id est furor.*"

The hanging described in the *Rúnatal* explains some of the aliases of Óðinn, like *Geiguðr* ("he who hangs"), Hangi ("the hung one") or Skollvaldr (the "lord of oscillation"). In skaldic poetry, gallows are often called "the

---

5 Françoise Bader, *La langue des dieux ou l'hermétisme des poètes indoeuropéens*, Giardini, Pise 1988, p. 41. But see also Edgar C. Polomé's criticism, "Inspiration, connaissance, magie ou voyance. La fonction fondamentale du dieu *Wôðan(az) et l'étymologie de son nom," in *Incognita*, 1991, pp. 32–47.

6 *Les Indo-Européens*, op. cit., p. 387.

hung's horse." Óðinn is indeed the god of the hung (*hangatýr*, Handagud), the "lord of gallows" (*galga valdr*) and "hanging seems to have been a typical way to offer him sacrifices."[7] In the *Hávamál* (str. 157), he is also said to have the power to bring back to like the hung by inscribing and coloring runes for them (*svá ec ríst oc í rúnom fác*).

---

7   Renauld-Krantz, *Structures de la mythologie nordique*, G. P. Maisonneuve and Larose, Paris 1962, pp. 63–64.

20

Runic Magic in Sagas — The Runesmith

ICELANDIC SAGAS MENTION RUNIC magic several times. Grettir's Saga (*Grettis saga Ásmundarsonar*) narrates how the old witch Þuríðr engraved evil runes: "She took her knife and engraved runes in the root [of the tree], she colored them red with her blood and performed incantations" (Chapter 79).

Egill's Saga (*Egils saga Skalla-Grímssonar*) which is usually attributed to Snorri Sturluson narrates that its hero was not only versed in the art of skalding, but also knew the secrets of the runes and used them for magical, preventive or therapeutic purposes. In Chapter 72, Egill Skallagrímsson finds a young girl on a farm who suffers from lethargy. A young man had unsuccessfully tried to heal her by clumsily engraving "love runes" (*manrúnar*) on a baleen that he put under her bed. Egill sees that the runes were poorly written and gently scratches them, burns the chips and declares: "None shall engrave runes / If one can't discern them" (*Skalat maðr rúnar rista, / nema ráða vel kunni*). Then he picks up his knife, cuts his palm and engraves some other runes, which enable the sick girl to quickly lose her lethargy: "I engrave the rune in the whalebone. / I color the characters red with blood / I choose my words / To engrave them in the whalebone."[1]

---

1 *La Saga de Egil Skallagrimsson. Histoire poétique d'un Viking scandinave du Xe siècle*, Office de publicité, Bruxelles 1925, p. 99, translation F. Wagner. We also go by

"Other Norse works," writes François-Xavier Dillmann, "are just as rich in stories involving magic or divination."[2]

Egill Skalla-Grímsson is introduced in the saga that bears his name as a true "runesmith." That term is present as is in several runic inscriptions, like the one on the Björketorp Runestone (Sweden, 6th century): *haidRrūnō ronu falhk hādra ginrūnaR*, "I, runesmith, hide here powerful runes." The runesmith (*rúnameistari* in Icelandic medieval sources) is quite evidently the one who has the knowledge of the *Fuþark*, which isn't necessarily the case of the person actually engraving runes (*runristare* in Swedish, *Runenritzer* in German). But we know very little about his social status, his exact function or the circumstances he intervened under. It is possible that he had a sacerdotal function. "The vast majority of the twenty-five runesmiths whose names are mentioned in writing is made of magicians, consecrated beings, even priests," notes François-Xavier Dillmann.[3] Runesmiths could also be women. For that matter, Egill Skalla-Grímsson was raised by a woman versed in magic, just like the power of the runes was revealed to Sigurdr by the Valkyrie Sigrdrífa. Lastly, runesmiths could be poets: for instance, the Hillersjö stone (11th century) reads "The skald Torbjörn engraved runes," which is also the case of Egill Skalla-Grímsson. "The mastery of the runes gave the runesmith godlike powers [...] so the runesmith appears to be acting in the name of Odin himself, who invented

---

Françoix-Xavier Dillmann's translation ("Les runes dans la littérature noroise," art. cit., p. 59). For the original text, see *Egils saga Skalla-Grímssonar*, ed. by Sigurður Nordal, Hið Íslenzka Fornritafélag, Reykjavik 1933. See also Felix Genzmer, "Die Geheimrunen der Egilssaga," in *Arkiv för nordisk filologi*, 1952, pp. 39–47.

2 *Les magiciens dans l'Islande ancienne*, op. cit., p. 5. See also Carla Del Zotto and Giulia Piccaluga (ed.), *Religione e magia nelle saghe nordiche*, special issue of the *Studi e materiali di storia delle religioni*, July–December 2012.

3 "Tripartition fonctionnelle et écriture runique en Scandinavie à l'époque païenne," art. cit., p. 251. See also, from the same author, "Le maître-des-runes. Essai de détermination socio-anthropologique. Quelques réflexions méthodologiques," in Clairborne W. Thompson (ed.), *Proceedings of the First International Symposium on Runes and Runic Inscriptions*, op. cit., pp. 27–36; Fred Wulf, "Runenmeisternamen," in James E. Knirk (ed.), *Proceedings of the Third International Symposium on Runes and Runic Inscriptions*, Uppsala Universitet, Uppsala 1994, pp. 31–43; "Runenmeister," in Heinrich Beck, Dieter Geuenich and Heiko Steuer (ed.), *Reallexikon der Germanischen Altertumskunde*, vol. 25, op. cit.

the runes and gave them their magical powers," underlines Ludwig Buisson, citing the Noleby runestone.[4]

Runesmiths engrave "power runes." But even if several authors easily acknowledge that runes were used to engrave magical inscriptions, as we've seen, they readily claim that they aren't inherently magical. Yet, if we go by the Poetic Edda, it seems like the opposite. The *Rígsþula* poem, for instance, specifically maintains that mastering runic writing grants specific powers. In the *Sigrdrífumál* (the "Tales of Sigrdrífa") the Valkyrie Sigrdrífa gives to Sigurdr, who just woke up from his magical slumber, directives on how to use the runes: "If you need to know the fighting runes / If you want to be smart / You must engrave them in the pommel of the sword / Across the whole blade / and close to the tip / And mention Týr twice (*ok nefna tysvar Tý*)."[5] Then, in verses 6 to 19, she lists a whole set of runes (she calls them "true letters") responsible for powers: victory runes (*sigrúnar*), healing runes (*bótrúnar*), power runes (*meginrúnar*), saving runes (*bjargrúnar*), beer runes, backwash runes, memory runes, speech runes, limb runes, birthing runes, runes protecting from adultery, etc.[6] All those runes seem to actually hold a power within themselves.

---

4   Ludwig Buisson, *Der Bildstein Ardre VIII auf Gotland. Göttermythen, Heldensagen und Jenseitsglauben der Germanen im 8. Jahrhundert n. Chr.*, Vandenhoeck u. Ruprecht, Göttingen 1976, p. 17.

5   The rune seventeen, ↑ (**tīwaz*), is Týr's rune, the only god we are positive that a rune was named after. But **tīwaz* can also mean "god" in the general sense (*tivar* is the plural of *týr* in Old Scandinavian). See Anders Hultgård, "Ziu-Týr. Religionsgeschichtliche," in *Reallexikon der Germanischen Altertumskunde*, vol. 35, Walter de Gruyter, Berlin 2007, pp. 929–932.

6   *L'Edda poétique*, op. cit., pp. 625–627, translation by Régis Boyer.

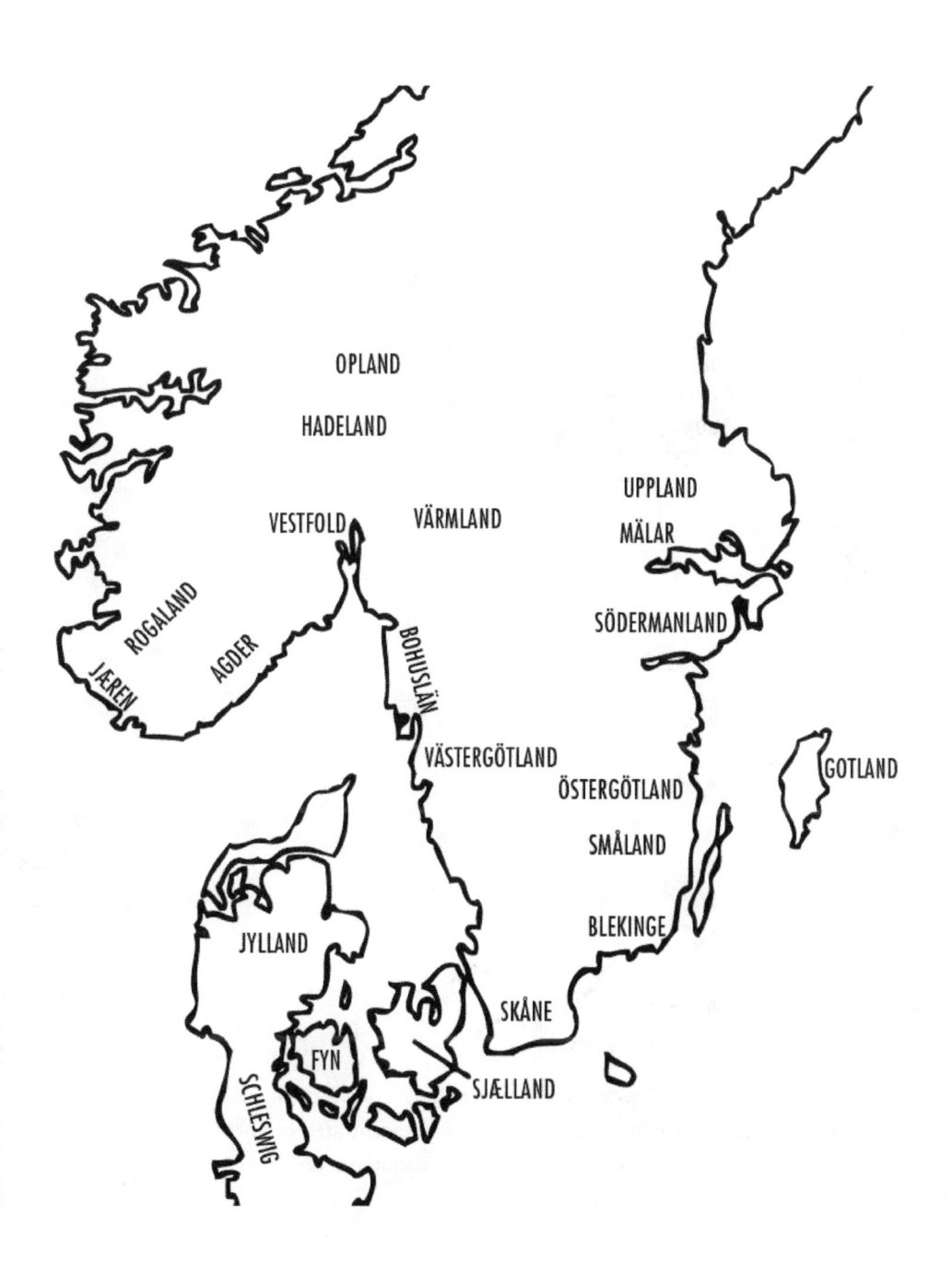

THE MAJOR RUNIC SITES in Scandinavia.

MAP OF THE SITES where most of the oldest known runic inscriptions have been found. It's easy to notice that they are concentrated in northern Europe, especially in Denmark and in southern Sweden.

PART III

21

The Three Phases of the Moon

THE SYMBOLIC OR MAGICAL CHARACTER of the runes tend to confirm that they were used for divinatory purposes before writing purposes, but it doesn't entirely explain the peculiar order of the *Fuþark* nor grouping the runes into three *ættir*. In order to better understand either one of those issues, we can only rely on theories. The theories we will expand on in this section, which are based on a number of consistent clues, in that the three sequences of eight runes originally corresponded to the three phases of the moon. The *Fuþark* is made of twenty-four signs partitioned into three eight-sign sequences, just like the Moon cycles through three sequences of eight nights (ascending moon, full moon, descending moon), and five moonless nights (or "black moon" nights). Is that similarity only a coincidence? We don't have to think so. It is only a theory, but many signs tell us to dig deeper.

Diodorus Siculus reminds us that, "in ancient times, when the Sun's motion was not understood, the year was counted thanks to the Moon's journey" (I, 25). There is also a consensus that the Moon's cycle was used by human societies to record time in the beginning, not the Sun's, since the former is simpler to track.[1] A solar year is 365.242 days, a lunar year is 354.367

---

1   See Daniel McLean McDonald, *The Origins of Metrology. Collected Papers*, McDonald Institute for Archaeological Research, Cambridge 1992.

days. A solar month is 30.436 days, a lunar month is 29.530 in average (the variation is the result of the orbit of the Moon around the Earth not being circular). Since a lunar year is about eleven days "late" compared to a solar year, the only way to correct the gap is to align the lunar year with the cycle of seasons and use leap days or months. That is the origin of the "twelve holy nights" (*Weihenächten, wihen nechten* in Middle High German, see *Weihnacht* "Christmas" in German), following the winter solstice for the Germanic people, or which correspond to the twelve days spent by Zeus (diurnal Sky) at Poseidon's (in "Ethiopia") for the Greeks, and to the twelve days of creative slumber of the Ṛbhus at Savitar and Agohya's for Vedic India (see also the Brahman ritual called *dvādaśāha* "the twelve-day sacrifice").

Alexander Marshack's work in America and Boris A. Frolov's work in Russia[2] have established in a parallel but independent way that the astronomical tracking of the Moon goes back to the Upper Paleolithic (30,000–10,000 BC). The Venus of Laussel, which is associated with the Gravettian Upper Paleolithic culture (approximately 25,000 years old), holds in its right hand a cornucopia decorated with thirteen vertical lines indicating the number of lunar circles that take place in a year. A Neolithic calendar discovered in the village of Slatino, Bulgaria, also displays a table with rows of vertical lines that indicate the phases of the Moon. It has been confirmed by archaeology, iconography and its role in winter nights that the cult of the Moon was present in Scandinavia in the Mesolithic.[3]

Thanks to microphotography and the use of binocular magnifying glasses, Alexander Marshack has been able to decipher marks and notches on several hundreds of prehistoric objects that go back to the Aurignacian and the Magdalenian (around the middle of the last Würm glaciation). Those marks and notches were until then considered to be "kill notches" or simply decorations, but they actually correspond to lunar phrasing notated with all its subdivisions. Among those objects, there is a 35,000-year-old small fragment exhumed from the Blanchard shelter in Dordogne, which bears sixty-nine round or crescent-shaped incisions which represent the phases of the Moon. Similar marks have been found on a reindeer antler from the

---

2   Boris A. Frolov, *Numbers in Paleolithic Graphics*, Nauka, Novosibirsk 1974.
3   See Patrick Ettighoffer, *Le Soleil et la Lune dans le paganisme scandinave, du mésolithique à l'âge du bronze récent (de 8000 à 500 av. J.-C.)*, L'Harmattan, Paris 2012.

Magdalenian period in the cave of La Marche, in Lussac-les-Châteaux, on bone and stone objects from the Lartet shelter (Dordogne), Niaux, Cougnac and Rouffignac in France, El Castillo and La Pileta in Spain. Marshack writes that

> it seems that as far back as 30,000 BC, during an ice age, the western-European hunter used an already evolved and complex notation system, whose tradition could have gone back several thousand years. [...] [Those notations] weren't a writing like we understand it to be yet. Nonetheless, it does seem like we could see in it the roots of science and writing, insofar as we have archaeological testimonies which indicate in all likelihood the presence of cognitive processes which will show up later on in science and writing.[4]

He also notes about a lunar calendar engraved on the mattock of Urgerlöse (Denmark):

> That calendar could explain the presence of a tradition of notation and observation in northern and central Europe at a time when the faraway agricultural cultures of the South had a different regional tradition. It could explain the origin of calendar sticks and runic calendars found in northern Europe in the modern period.

The coincidence between women's menstrual periods and the length of the lunar cycle has of course been noticed very early on. It explains why the (full) moon has often been considered to be a symbol of fecundity. The words for "month" and for "moon" are related in many Indo-European languages, including English and *Monat* and *Mond* in German. See also *arma-* "moon, month" in Hittite, *mañ* "month" in Tocharian A, *mēnsis*

---

[4] Alexander Marshack, *The Roots of Civilization. The Cognitive Beginnings of Man's First Art, Symbol and Notation*, McGraw-Hill, New York 1972 (French Translation: *Les racines de la civilisation. Les sources cognitives de l'art, du symbole et de la notation chez les premiers hommes*, Plon, 1973, pp. 57–58). See also "Cognitive Aspects of Upper Paleolithic Engraving," in *Current Anthropology*, June–October 1972, pp. 445–477; "Upper Paleolithic Notation and Symbols," in Science, 24 November 1972, pp. 817–828; "Upper Paleolithic Symbol Systems of the Russian Plain: Cognitive and Comparative Analysis," in *Current Anthropology*, June 1979, pp. 271–311; "On Paleolithic Ochre and the Early Uses of Color and Symbol," in *Current Anthropology*, April 1981, pp. 188–191; "Concepts théoriques conduisant à de nouvelles méthodes analytiques, de nouveaux procédés de recherche et catégories de données," in *L'Anthropologie*, 1984, 4, pp. 573–586.

"month" in Latin, *mí* (derived from **mensos*) "month" in Old Irish, *amis* "month" in Armenian. In Homeric Greek, the word for moon is *meí*, *mès* in the Dorian dialect, and *mèn* in classical Greek, which also means "month."[5] See also the names of the Greek goddess Mēnē, the Gaul goddess Mene, the Armenian goddess Amins. All those words are derived from the Indo-European **me(n)s-*.[6] "Comparative philology shows than in Indo-European languages, the terms that designate the month and the moon are identical, with possibly some small different suffixes, so we can deduce that at the time of the first Aryans, the month was determined by the moon."[7] That lunar month is split into three eight- or nine-night periods corresponding to the phases of the moon.

"Like many other Neolithic peoples," writes Jean Haundry, "the Indo-Europeans started counting years with twelve lunar months (they could even have initially started with ten-month years!)." Lokmanya Bāl Gangādhar Tilak notes that Indo-Europeans "made offerings every morning and evening, every new and full moon."[8] Tacitus relates in Chapter 11 of his *Germania* that the Germanic people gathered at the beginning of lunar cycles or when the moon was full:

> unless an untimely and sudden event happened, they gathered on specific days, during new or full moons (*quum aut inchoatur luna aut impletur*), because they believe that there can't be a better influence to deal with matters at hand.[9]

He adds that unlike the Romans, the Germanic people don't measure time in days but in nights because to them, nights are more important than days: "Moreover, they do not count time with days, like we do, but with nights, and

---

5   In Latin, *mensis* only means "month," the name of the moon (*luna*) come from somewhere else.

6   In Indo-European, the moon is also called **louksna* "the bright." See Anton Scherer, *Gestirnnamen bei den indogermanischen Völkern*, Carl Winter, Heidelberg 1953.

7   Jean Haudry, "Notes sur les racines indo-européennes **mē-*, **met-*, **med-* 'mesurer'," in *Etudes indo-européennes*, XI, 1992, p. 47.

8   Lokmanya Bāl Gangādhar Tilak, *Orion ou recherches sur l'antiquité des Védas*, Archè, Milano 1989, p. 29. In Germanic, the name of the moon (**mēnan-*) became differentiated from the month, which kept its original form (**mēnōþ-*).

9   *La Germanie. L'origine et le pays des Germains*, op. cit., p. 27, translation Patrick Voisin.

that is that principle that guides their appointments and summons, because for them, days begin after the end of the night,"[10] Bede the Venerable also writes in 725 in his *De Temporum Ratione* that the Anglo-Saxons counted time according to the course of the Moon: "*antiqui autem Anglorum populi* [...] *iuxta cursum lunæ suos menses computauere.*"[11] Traces of that period can still be found in German expressions or terms like *Sonnabend, heiliger Abend, Weihnachtsabend*. The German word for "week," *Woche* (*wiko* in Gothic, *weka* in Old High German, *wika* in Old Norse, *wike* or *wuku* in Anglo-Saxon, *wike* in Frisian) originally means change (*Wechsel*), that is going from one phase of the moon to another. The word *heute* "today" is derived from **hiu dagu* meaning "this day" in Germanic, singular instrumental case of **hi- dag(a)*, but there's also *hinaht*, "this night" in Old High German.[12]

Caesar said about the Gauls the following: "They do not count days, but nights; birthdays, the beginnings of months and years are counted by making the day start with the night" (*De bello gallico*, VI, 18). According to Pliny the Elder, Gallic months started on the sixth day of the moon (*Natural Historye*, XVI, 250). The starting point of the year was the *samionos* full moon. In Old Irish, there are two words for "week," *sehtuin* (*sechtmain*) is a recent word translating the Latin *septimana*, and *nouas* (**nevm-etā*) which means "nine nights" is an older one, which confirms the existence of a nine-night measurement unit for time before the week. In Welsh, another

---

10 Ibid., p. 39. Original text: "*Nec dierum numerum ut nos, sed noctium computant; sic constituunt, sic condicunt; nos ducere diem videtur.*" In Pierre Grimal's translation: "Because to them, the night shows the path to daylight." ("Les mœurs des Germains," in Tacitus, *Œuvres choisies*, op. cit., pp. 38). The verb computare means here "to count, to calculate" (see the words *computatio* or *computus* from medieval Latin, hence "comput").

11 See Kenneth Harrison, *The Framework of Anglo-Saxon History to A.D. 900*, Cambridge University Press, Cambridge 1976 ("The moon and the Anglo-Saxon calendar," pp. 1–14).

12 See also *fortnight*, derived from Old English *fēowertyne niht*, "fourteen days," the average interval between a full moon and a new moon. Its Irish equivalent is *coicis*. The French expression "quinze jours," which designates two seven-day weeks, is found in Spanish, Portuguese, Italien, Catalan and also Greek (*dekapenthímero*). In Welsh, the term *pymthefnos* means "fifteen nights," the name of a week being *wythnos*, literally "eight nights." See also the expression "in eight days" (In German: "*in acht Tage*"), meaning "in a week."

word for week is *wythnos* "eight nights." In Breton, the word for morrow is *antronoz*. The habit of counting with nights and not days is also confirmed for ancient Greeks, especially in Athens. The expression "night and day" is more frequent than "day and night" in Homer's work.

The famous lunisolar Coligny calendar, found in 189 near Bourg (AIN) on a territory formerly occupied by the Gallic Ambarri also confirms the importance of the Moon for the Celts. Dating from the 1st or 2nd century, this large slab of bronze -of which subsists 153 fragments- indicates the succession of days and months on a five-year timespan (so around 1835 days). All the words on it are written in Gaulish. The calendar is made up of thirty-day months (MAT, *matu*) that are considered to be positive, and twenty-nine-day months (ANMATV, *anmatu*) that are considered to be negative. Leap months are used to standardize the lunar calendar and the solar cycle. Every month is divided into a first period of fifteen days and a second period of fourteen or fifteen days. That division is often marked by the word ATENOVX (**atenocts*) "ascending night," "return of the moon" or "darkness once again" (See *athnughudh* which means "resurgence" in Middle Irish). There is also the TRINUX or TRINOX distinction, meaning "three nights" (*trinoxtion Samoni sindiu* "celebration of the three nights of Samonios today").[13]

The ancient ten month and thirty-eight-week Roman calendar called "Romulus's calendar" (as opposed to Numa's reformed calendar), which made the year start in March, is affected by the lunar cycle, as the division of months into calends, nones ("nine day timespans") and ides show. The calends, which designate the first day of the month, corresponded to the

---

13 On the Coligny calendar, see Françoise Le Roux, Christian-J. Guyonvarc'h and Jord Pinault, "Le calendrier gaulois de Coligny (Ain)," in *Ogam*, 1961, pp. 635–660; Paul-Marie Duval and Georges Pinault, "Observations sur le calendrier de Coligny," in *Etudes celtiques*, 1962, 10, pp. 18–42 and 372–412, 11, pp. 7–45 and 269–313; Jean-Paul Parisot, "Les phases de la lune et les saisons dans le calendrier de Coligny," in *Etudes indo-européennes*, 13, June 1985, pp. 1–18; Paul-Marie Duval and Georges Pinault, *Recueil des inscriptions gauloises (III). Les calendriers (Coligny, Villards d'Héria)*, Éditions du CNRS, Paris 1986; Garrett S. Olmsted, The Gaulish Calendar, Rudolf Habelt, Bonn 1992; Garrett S. Olmsted, *A Definitive Reconstructed Text of the Coligny Calendar*, Institute for the Study of Man, Washington 2001; Jean-Michel Le Contel and Paul Verdier, *Un calendrier celtique. Le calendrier gaulois de Coligny*, Errance, Paris 1997. See also Joseph Monard, *Astronymie et onomastique calendaire celtiques. Le ciel et l'année chez les Celte*s, Label LN, Ploudalmézeau 2005.

new moon. The ides corresponded to the full moon. "None" designated the ninth day before the ides. In Rome, the nundines (*nundinæ*) were market days that took place every eight days in the calendar, thereby separating weeks (the interval between nundines was called *nundinum*). Some special ceremonies took place during calends, nones and ides, and all three of those "were linked to the phases of the moon and derived from a very ancient time when people used a lunar calendar."[14] The ides were devoted to Jupiter. Weeks were eight days long, but they likely used to be nine nights long. The tradition gives the credit for the introduction of the eight days long week to the Etruscans. *Nundinæ* and *nonæ*, which have the same etymology, probably originally had the same meaning before the nones became the ninth day before the ides. Macrobius (I, 16, 36) mentioned a divinity called Nundina, which presided over the day when babies are named, the ninth after a boy's birth and the eighth after a girl's birth. One can find that Germanic people also had a rite to recognize a child and giving it a name on its ninth day, especially in *Lex Salica* and *Lex Ribuaria* ("*infra novem noctibus*"), as well as the Visigoths and the Alamanni.

The oldest Greek calendar was also a lunar calendar that divided the year in two. Every month was divided in three phases corresponding to the ascending moon, the full moon, and descending moon. A leap month was periodically added.

So, there is no doubt that the lunar cycle was the first to have been used to measure time, and that it was the observation of the phases of the moon that made it possible. The first day of the week is incidentally always Monday (*Montag* in German, *dilun* in Breton, etc.), meaning the "day of the moon." In many Indo-European languages, the name of the moon also means "splitter" or "time measuring," the Indo-European root of its name being *meH_1 "to measure" (see *mā-* in Old Indian, *mā-* in Avestan, *ētīrī* in Latin "to measure," *métron* in Greek "measurement," *messen* in German "to measure"), which shows that "measurements" originally applied especially to measuring time. As a *Zeitmesser* or *Zeitteiler*, the moon splits time and partitions the year (see *metai* "year" in Lithuanian). It is even echoed in the

---

14 See H. H. Scullard, *Festivals and Ceremonies of the Roman Republic*, Thames & Hudson, London 1981, p. 43.

Bible, where it reads that Yahweh "made the moon to mark the seasons" (Psalms 104, 19). In the Poetic Edda, "Alvíss's tale" (*Alvíssmál*) specifies that the moon is called *máni* by men and *mýlinn* by gods, and that "elves" (álfar) call it year-counter" (*ártali*, str. 14). Jean Haundry writes:

> From the reflection on the monthly cycle begot a rich lunar mythology that shouldn't be rejected, even if it has sometimes been used inconsistently [...] the Moon god is probably the oldest warrior god of the Indo-Europeans [...] the Moon is de facto the only major celestial body that doesn't fear venturing into the nocturnal sky, realm of demons and spirits of the dead. Moreover, before being able to calculate the lunisolar year, Indo-Europeans, like many other peoples, used the lunar year. So, the monthly cycle and the moon god are closely linked since the origin of the annual cycle.[15]

---

15 Jean Haudry, *La religion cosmique des Indo-Européens*, Archè, Milano, and Belles Lettres, Paris 1987, p. 290. Cf. also Otto Schrader, *Die älteste Zeittheilung des indogermanischen Volkes*, Carl Habel, Berlin 1878; Eduard Stucken, *Der Ursprung des Alphabetes und die Mondstationen*, J. C. Hinrichs, Leipzig 1913; Wolfgang Schultz, *Zeitrechnung und Weltordnung in ihren übereinstimmenden Grundzügen bei den Indern, Iraniern, Hellenen, Italikern, Kelten, Germanen, Litauern, Slawen*, Curt Kabitzsch, Leipzig 1924.

22

Eight and Nine

MAURICE CAHEN SAID THAT "the partition [of the *Fuþark*] into three groups seems to be the result of magical preoccupations," especially since "the number 'eight' has a special place in runic magic."[1] Ralph W. V. Elliot believes it is likely that "the numbers three and eight played a part in the magical usage of the runes."[2] The number nine must be added to those two numbers, which is a superlative amplification of the number three (3 x 3). Indeed, everywhere they are found, the number eight and nine seem to have a connection with the phases of the moon and with the night.

Examining the vocabulary brings about a curious assessment right away. In most Indo-European languages, except Slavic languages, the number eight and the term for "night" (from Indo-European **nokwt-s* "night") are related, the word for night being an equivalent of eight with an "n"-prefix.

FRENCH: *huit / nuit*
OLD FRENCH: *oit — uit / noit — nuit*
OLD HIGH GERMAN: *ahtō / naht*
MIDDLE HIGH GERMAN: *ahte / nacht*
GOTHIC: *ahtau / nahts*

---

1   "Origine et développement de l'écriture runique," art. cit., pp. 16–17.
2   *Runes. An Introduction*, op. cit., p. 14.

22. EIGHT AND NINE

GERMAN: *acht / Nacht*
ENGLISH: *eight / night*
DUTCH: *acht / nacht*
SWEDISH: *åtta (ōtta) / natt*
NORWEGIAN: *åtte / natt*
DANISH: *otte / nat*
OLD ENGLISH: *eahta — æhta / niht — nieht*
LATIN: *octo / nox, nocto*
ITALIAN: *otto / notte*
SPANISH: *ocho / noche*
PORTUGUESE: *oito / noite*
CATALAN: *vuit / nit*
OCCITAN: *uèch / nuèch*
ROMANIAN: *opt / noapte*
BRETON: *eizh / noz*

Furthermore, in almost all Indo-European languages, the number nine is a homonym or the quasi-homonym of the adjective "new."

FRENCH: *neuf / neuf*
GERMAN: *neun / neu*
DUTCH: *negen / nieuw*
NORWEGIAN: *ni / ny*
DANISH: *ni / ny*
ENGLISH: *nine / new*
LATIN: *novem / novus*
ITALIAN: *nove / nuovo*
SPANISH: *nueve / nuevo*
PORTUGUESE: *nove / novo*
CATALAN: *nou / nou*
ROMANIAN: *noua / nou*
BRETON: *naw or nav / nevez*

How should those two series be interpreted, knowing that they seem to be too systematic to be a coincidence? What is the link between eight and "night?" And what novelty corresponds to a pace of nine? "Nine" here can not be interpreted as a symbol of human gestation, since people only knew lunar months and a pregnancy lasts ten lunar months (280 days according to the lunar calendar) or nine solar months. The only conceivable answer is that nine marks the transition from one phase of the moon to another: nine happens at the end of a set of eight nights. However, it should be noted that according to Václav Blažek, the Indo-European numeral eight has the form *$H_2oktoH_1(u)$ and it means "the two tips" (fingers without the two thumbs). The same author states that *H_1newm *H_1en-H_1newm apply to nine and mean "lacking" (it lacks one compared to ten). The initial laryngeal then supposedly diverted from the *$néwo$- "new" group.[3]

Moreover, the figure nine is especially important in the Germanic religion. Earlier in this book, we've talked about how Óðínn hangs for "nine nights" from Yggdrasill and how the giant Bölthorn then teaches him nine "mighty songs" (*Hávamál*, str. 138-140). In the *Grímnismál*, after having taken the appearance of *Grímnir*, he consents to being detained for eight days and eight nights by the king Geirrödr, and then he kills him on the ninth night after having revealed his true identity. He owns a golden ring called Draupnir (literally the "drier"), which significantly multiplies itself eight times every nine nights (*Skírnismál*, str. 21) — a clear allusion to the

---

3 See also J. P. Mallory and D. Q. Adams, *The Oxford Introduction to Proto-Indo-European and the Proto-Indo-European World*, Oxford University Press, Oxford 2006 ("Basic Numerals," pp. 308–317). It should be noted that Ernst Jünger was also intrigued by that coincidence. In his journal "years of occupation," on the 11th of April 1948, it reads: "I remembered Kükelhaus's allusion to the strange fact that when one adds the n- of negation to it [the number eight], it becomes in many languages the word 'night,' Nacht, nox, night, nuit, notte and so on. Hence the following combination: according to linguists, in all Indo-European languages, the word for eight goes back to a common root which is the dual of 'four.' This invites us to conceive of a base four system, like it is still present in some contemporary cultures. *Eight* is the end of the road. And it is conceivable that there could have been an ancient connection between 'end' and 'night.' When reaching 'nine,' the count starts again, which would explain the striking relation there is in many languages between 'nine' and 'new,' neun and neu" (*La cabane dans la vigne. Journal IV, 1945–1948*, Christian Bourgois, Paris 1980, pp. 292-293. "Kükelhaus" here refers to the philosopher, pedagogue and craftsman Hugo Kükelhaus (1900-1984).

succession of the phases of the moon. Óðinn is also mentioned in the Anglo-Saxon poem *Nine Herbs Charm* where, armed with nine wands that probably bear runes, he prevails over a snake and cuts it into nine pieces.[4]

Nordic cosmology comprises nine worlds propped up by the cosmic tree Yggdrasill, whose roots dig deep to into the Earth. In the *Skírnismál* (str. 39–41), Freyr must wait nine nights before he can consummate his union with Gerðr. In the *Svipdagsmál*, the witch Gróa gives nine charms to her son Svipdag. In the same poem, nine servants sit with Menglöð. The god Hermódr rode Sleipnir for nine nights in order to save Baldr from Hel, the underworld (*Gylfaginning*, Chapter 49). The god Njördr and his wife Skadi, who quarrelled over where they would live, decided in the end to spend nine nights in at Þrymheimr and nine nights at Nóatún (*Gylfaginning*, Chapter 23).[5] Heimdallr was supposedly conceived by nine virgin sisters (*Gylfaginning*, Chapter 27). The *Skáldskaparmál* (Chapter 2) also mention that Óðinn made nine of Baugi's serfs kill each other. In the Edda, there's also mention of the nine daughters of giants (*Hyndluljód*, str. 35), the nine heads of Þrivaldi, the nine daughters of Ægir, etc.

We know from Adam of Bremen, who wrote from around 1080, that the largest ceremonies at the pagan temple of Uppsala took place every nine years (*post novem annos*), that they were in honor of Óðinn, Þórr and Freyr, and that they lasted nine days.[6] Traditional songs (*neniae*) were executed. René L. M. Derolez highlights on that topic that

---

4   See Godfrid Storms, *Anglo-Saxon Magic*, Martinus Nijhoff, The Hague 1948, pp. 188–189.

5   After having conducted the philological study of the four main manuscripts of the *Prose Edda*, François-Xavier Dillmann showed that it wasn't actually nine nights at one place and nine nights at the other place, like it is usually said to be, but nine nights at Njördr's, then three nights at Skadi's. The author compares that myth with the myth of Kore (Persephone), abducted by Hades in the different versions of the Homeric hymns. See his contribution, "Les nuits de Njördr et de Skadi. Notes critiques sur un chapitre de la *Snorra Edda*," in John Ole Askedal, Harald Bjorvand and Eyvind Fjeld Halvorsen (ed.), *Festskrift til Ottar Grønvik*, op. cit., pp. 174–182, and his translation of the Edda (*L'Edda. Récits de mythologie nordique*, Gallimard, Paris 1991, p. 55, and note p. 165). It should be noted that the god Njördr also has nine daughters, the eldest is called Rodhveig and the youngest is called Krippvör.

6   Adam of Bremen, *Gesta Hammaburgensis Ecclesiæ Pontificum*, IV, 26–27. For Otto Sigfrid Reuter (*Germanische Himmelskunde. Untersuchungen zur Geschichte des Geistes*, J. F. Lehmanns, München 1934), the expression *post novem annos* should rather be understood as meaning an eight-year cycle. According to the testimony of

Ljungberg observed carefully the reactions of Swedish paganism against Christians. He noticed that the manifestations of animosity occured approximately every nine years (or in multiples of nine: around 1021, 1039, 1057, 1066, 1075, 1084, 1120), put another way, they very likely coincided with the celebrations that took place in Uppsala every nine years.[7]

Were those nine years originally lunar years? In any case, a homology between the nine-day lunar cycle and periods corresponding to nine lunar months or nine lunar years is probable.

Among the Celts, the king Lóegaire surrounds himself with nine chariots "in accordance with the gods' tradition." Ysbaddaden Bencawr's castle has nine gates, nine gatekeepers and nine watchdogs. King Arthur fights in vain the Twrch Trwyth during nine nights and nine days. According to the *Vita Merlini*, nine sisters stay up in the isle of fruit, the equivalent of Avalon, and the main one is Morgan. There are also nine plains and nine rivers created by the Dagda, nine sisters attacking Samson on his journey in Wales, nine witches between Peredur and Caer Loyw, etc.

In Greece, Demeter travels the world for nine days looking for her daughter Persephone, abducted by Hephaestus. Leto, the embodiment of the Night, suffers during nine days and nine nights from giving birth. The nine Muses, daughters of Zeus and Mnemosyne (whose names are Clio, Calliope, Melpomene, Thalia, Euterpe, Erato, Terpsichore, Polyhymnia and Urania) are born after nine nights of love-making. Tradition dictates that it took Minos nine years in his cave to receive Jupiter's laws. Another legend states that Minos had a meeting with Jupiter every nine years, after which he could prophesy. Every nine years, Athens sent to Crete seven young men and seven young girls to sacrifice to the Minotaur. In Homer's work, Ulysses attributes nine goats to the crew manning his twelve ships. In Pylos, every group of 500 men, sitting on nine benches, offered nine steers to Poseidon, etc.

---

the chronicler Thietmar of Merseburg (975–1018), solemn sacrifices also took place every nine years in Lethra, Zeeland (*Chronicon Thietmari Merseburgensis*).

7   *Les dieux et la religion des Germains*, op. cit., p. 247. The book the author mentions is Helge Ljungberg's, *Den nordiska religionen och kristendomen. Studier över det nordiska religionsskiftet under vikingatiden*, H. Geber, Stockholm 1938.

23

The Norns, the Parcae and the Moirai

THE POEM KNOWN AS Völuspá (the "clairvoyant's prediction") is one of the most beautiful sacred poems of medieval pagan literature. In it, the *völva* or clairvoyant (the female substantive spá originally refers to a vision, see *speculum* in Latin) vaticinates on the great events of the history of the universe. This sixty-six-verse poem has been recorded around the middle of the 13th century in the Codex Regius (which is written in Old Norse and only contains sixty-two verses), and the *Hauksbók* (sixty-six verses). Around 1230, Snorri Sturluson used many excerpts of it in the *Gylfaginning*. The original text seems to have been written at the end of the 10th century by an anonymous poet based on much more ancient sources. In the sixth verse, the *völva* proclaims:

> So all the gods rose up
> To sit on the judgment seats,
> Supreme divinities,
> And they conferred;
> Gave names to
> The night and the descending moon,
> They named the morning
> And the middle of the day,
> The fresh and brown
> And counted time in years.[1]

---

1 *L'Edda poétique*, op. cit., p. 533, translation by Régis Boyer.

This text shows how important the "night" and the "descending moon" are to the Æsir gods, who gave them names, and also how important it is to "count time in years" to them. So, it confirms the role the lunar cycle had in measuring time. But the *Völuspá* also mentions the three Norns, who are considered to be "virgins learned in many things" and who dwell under Yggdrasill's foliage, the cosmic tree which remains "eternally green":

> One is named Urdr,
> The other, Verdandi,
> — chopped logs —,
> Skuld, the third one;
> They created the laws,
> They established the lives
> of the children of men
> and the mortals' fate.[2]

The name Urd means "what once was" (the past), Verdandi means "what is, what it becomes" (the present), and Skuld means "what will be" (the future). The three Norns (*norn*, plural *nornir*) are akin to the Dísir, who regulate the fate of the dwellers of the nine worlds of Nordic cosmogony. They are the "spinners" crafting the thread of men's fate.[3] The text says that they "chopped logs" (*scáro á scíði*). "Maybe it is an allusion to the art of engraving runes," comments Régis Boyer.[4] It should then be translated: "They engraved in wood."

As divinities of fate, the three Norns are the Germanic equivalent to the Greek Moirai and the Roman Parcae. In the Greek religion, the Moirai are daughters of Zeus and Hera and live in a place next to where the Horae live. In Hesiod's Theogony (v. 215), they are significantly introduced as the daughters of the Night, which confirms that they correspond to the three phases of the moon. Incidentally, the word *moira* means "phase." Clotho, the "spinner" is linked to the new moon and the spring, Lachesis, the

---

2   Ibid., p. 537.

3   See François-Xavier Dillmann, "Nornen," in *Reallexikon der Germanische Altertumskunde*, 2nd ed., vol. 21, Walter de Gruyter, Berlin 2002, pp. 388–394; Karen Bek-Pedersen, *The Norns in Old Norse Mythology*, Dunedin Academic Press, Edinburgh 2011.

4   *L'Edda poétique*, op. cit., p. 217.

"alloter" (her name means "fate" or "action of drawing randomly") is linked to the full moon and the summer, Atropos, the "inevitable" is linked to the descending moon and the winter." The Romans called Clotho Nona, "the ninth," another hint for a link between the number nine and the "novelty" represented by the new moon. The "triple moon" (ascending, full and descending) might also correspond to the "triple Hékatè" or Tyndareus's three daughters: Helen, Phoebe and Clytmnestra (see also the three oracular priestesses in the Zeus sanctuary in Dodona). All of this clearly shows the connection between divination or foretelling, which required runes, and the phases of the moon which correspond to three series of eight nights.

24

The Homology Between Day and Year

JEAN HAUDRY SUGGESTED BRINGING together under the expression "cosmic religion of the Indo-Europeans" a "coherent group of representations coming from a reflection on the three main temporal cycles: the daily cycle of the day, night, dawn and twilight, the yearly cycle and the cosmic cycle, both built after the model set by the daily cycle."[1] Going back to the Mesolithic, if not the Paleolithic, when the life of men depended heavily on the cycle of seasons, this ancient cosmology comprised both a "diurnal sky" and a "nocturnal sky." Those two skies were separates by a "red sky," which is either a dawn sky and a crepuscular sky. The mythology and the divinities associated with those three skies primarily express the desire to go back to the sunnier season, which is considered to be the dawn of the year.

This approach sheds light on a more archaic stage of the Indo-European religion than the stage with the ideology of the three functions, while helping us to understand how it got to that stage. By giving a central importance to some cosmic entities, first and foremost the Ausōs (Eōs in Greek, Uṣas

---

1 *La religion cosmique des Indo-Européens*, op. cit., p. 1. See also Jean Haudry, "Les trois cieux," in *Etudes indo-européennes*, January 1982, pp. 23–48; "Les âges du monde, les trois fonctions et la religion cosmique des Indo-Européens," *in Etudes indo-européennes*, 1990, pp. 99–121.

in Indo-Aryan, *auróra* in Latin, *Austrō* in Old German), it explains the origin of the tripartite ideology by making the sovereign gods of the Indo-Europeans out to be representatives of the "diurnal sky" instead of "radiant" gods or simply "celestial gods,"[2] in opposition to the "nocturnal sky" which has its own divinities (**Tīwa-* for the Germanic, **Mitra-* for Vedic India). It also leads us towards analyzing the Indo-European concept of "year" as a "dual bank" entity, directly linked to the "heroic" theme of the "crossing of the dark wintery waters."

In this initial state of the Indo-European religion, the essential theme is the homology of the time units, which makes the cosmic cycle the homolog of the day and the year, each of those units being split in three phases, a descending phase and an ascending phase with a dawn or crepuscular phase in between the two (the year starts with the winter, just like the day starts with the night). This idea is especially present in ancient Indian literature. In the description of the divisions of time, it reads: "a mortal's year is a day and a night for the gods; and here is how the division is done: the day is the result of the sun going North and the night is the result of the sun going South" (*Manu*, I, 67). Likewise, in the *Taittirīya Brāhmana*: "What takes a year only takes a day for the gods." In the Indo-Iranian *Avesta*, the text of the *Vendidad* (I, 1–3) also has a passage where Ahura Mazda says that "in the Vara that Yima made," the inhabitants "consider that a day is like a year." This formulation, which can reflect the memory of an ancient arctic accommodation,[3] has a Greek and a Germanic equivalent. Therefore it is an inherited Indo-European formulation. "The system of three temporal cycles devised as homologues can be considered to be the central focus of the Indo-European idea of the conception of the world."[4]

In that system, the year is considered to have a diurnal part, a nocturnal part, a dawn and a twilight, in the image of the daily cycle. When it is not split in two periods, a bright ("diurnal" or spring-summer) one and a dark

---

2   The Proto-Indo-European word for "diurnal sky," **dyḗw-*, both led to the word for "sky" and for "day," and by extension to the word for "god" **deyw-ó-*, literally "of the diurnal sky." This etymon is also found in the names of *Jūpiter*, *Zeús*, the Vedic *Dyau* and the Irish *Dag-da*, who are originally deified diurnal skies.

3   See Lokamanya Bāl Gangādhar Tilak, *Origine polaire de la tradition védique. Nouvelles clés pour l'interprétation de nombreux textes et légendes védiques*, Archè, Milano 1979.

4   Jean Haudry, *La religion cosmique des Indo-Européens*, op. cit., p. 285.

("nocturnal" or wintery) one, it it is divided into three seasons, in the same way as the lunar month is divided into three periods of eight or nine nights.[5] This notion gives meaning to the union of Zeus, god of the diurnal sky, and Hera. Philippe Jouët writes:

> The Indo-European year was made of two parts, a summer part and a winter part, which were respectively considered to be diurnal and nocturnal and were present in the Celtic year. The Indo-Europeans had a goddess of the year, whose name was found by F. R. Schröder in the name of the Greek *Hera*. The couple *dyew-yērā-* (Zeus-Hera in Greek) mythologically represents the alliance of the Diurnal-Sky and the Summertime, whose hierogamy signals the springtime return of light.[6]

In the original Greek pantheon, Zeus is not in fact the spouse of the Earth, but the spouse (and brother) of the Year, Hera, who was originally the female embodiment of the summertime (this is why she is constantly associated with the color white). Likewise, Aphrodite represented the Dawn of the year before becoming the goddess of love. This is why the Vedic hymns dedicated to the Dawn must be understood both as a daily celebration of the sunrise (a function attributed later on to Eōs in Greece) and as a celebration of the end of wintertime. The Greeks also divided the year in seasons called *horae*, a name that first applied to the three yearly seasons, and then to the parts of the day, because hours constitute the "seasons" in a way. It is only after a long evolution, underlines Haudry, that the Hours' (*Horae*) name finally became the unit days were counted in. In the Iliad, where they are first mentioned, they are introduced as gatekeepers of the sky. Their "return" originally served the purpose of counting the years. According to Hesiod, they are named Eunomia, Dike and Eirene.

The Indo-Europeans refer to the "summertime" with the nominal theme *yē/ōr-*. This is the term that ended up meaning the entirety of the year (see

---

5 Tacitus confirms that the Germanic people knew only three seasons: spring, summer and winter.

6 Philippe Jouët, *Dictionnaire de la mythologie et de la religion celtiques*, Yoran embanner, Fouesnant 2012, p. 93. From the same author: *Etudes de symbolisme celtique. Rythmes et nombres*, Label LN, Ploudalmézeau 2012. Franz Rolf Schröder's article cited by Philippe Jouët was published in *Gymnasium*, LXVI, 1956, pp. 57 ff. The author demonstrates, in particular by using a notation in Mycenaean (*era*), that the name Hera comes from the old Indo-European word for year.

yār- in Avestan, *ar* in Danish, *år* in Swedish, *jēr* in Gothic, *jār* in Old High German, *Jahr* in German, *jēr* in Old Frisian, *jier* in Frisian, *jaer* in Middle Dutch, *jaar* in Dutch, *gēar* in Anglo-Saxon, *géar* or *gēr* in Old English, *year* in English, *jéras* in Lithuanian, etc. See also the Venetic word for year, confirmed in the inscriptions of Este, **yōro-*).[7] In Greece, the same term, in a revealing way, gave the Hours their name (**yōrā*), who are originally divinities associated with the return of the spring (they accompany the dawn of the year) and by extension the whole summertime, as well as Hera's name (**yērā-*), Zeus's spouse, and finally the term "hero," which originally is the person who "conquers the year," meaning the one who reaches or delivers the spring after having "crossed the waters of the wintery darkness" (see Heracles's name and Jaroslav's name, both meaning "glory of the summertime"). Jean Haundry writes:

> Inspections of mythological and ritual facts showed that the union [of Zeus and Hera] initially symbolized the yearly reunion of the summertime and the light of day after the wintery night, thereby enabling us to understand the well established — but inexplicable — homology between year and day: a mortal's year is a day for gods.[8]

---

7   On the Indo-European denominations for year, see also Lenka Dockalová and Václav Blažek, "The Indo-European Year," in *The Journal of Indo-European Studies*, autumn-winter 2011, pp. 414–495.

8   *La religion cosmique des Indo-Européens*, op. cit., p. 3. See also Jean Haudry, "Héra," in *Etudes indo-européennes*, 6, September 1983, pp. 17–46; "Héra (suite)," in *Etudes indo-européennes*, 7, February 1984, pp. 1–28; "Les Heures," in *Etudes indo-européennes*, 18, September 1986, pp. 1–14. In the Greek religion, Zeus is also the spouse of Leto, which represents the Night. This is confirmed by her Nychia epithet. From that union were birthed Artemis, a lunar divinity, and Apollo, a solar divinity. It should be noted that it took Leto to give birth (this is the yearly "long night") and that, on an inscription from Tenea, Apollo is said to be the "boss of the Hours" (*ōromédōn*).

25

The Rune for The Word "Year"

Jean Haudry writes that: "curiously, the Germanic rune for the year, the one designating the phoneme /j/ and named after the word *jēr(a) which means year, has the shape of a Janus,"[1] that is to say the dual-faced god who, in Rome, notably patronized the transition between years (his name is also found in the name of the month "January").

This rune is the rune number twelve, ᛃ or ᛡ (*jēran or *jæran, which are derived from *ieran but there are also the forms *jāra *jēra-, ár and ger), and it indicates the semi-vowel j. Made of two juxtaposed curves or semicircles, one being convex and the other concave, its meaning is both "(good) year" and "good times (season)," which corresponds to the dual meaning of its Indo-European root. Runic poems gloss ár with "bountiful harvest," a notion that is also found in ōra in Greek and jarŭ in Old Russian "spring, good

---

[1] Janus is actually made of the Indo-European divine fire, which explains his relationship with the Vesta. Haudry clarifies that his connection to the year "can be coming from an ancient homology like the one established by the Upanishads between the 'way of gods' and the ascending part of the year, the 'fathers' way'" ("La préhistoire de Janus," in *Revue des études latines*, 2005 [2006], p. 53). The link between Janus and the beginning of the astronomical year should be tied together with the link between the Latvian Janis and the summer solstice. See Jean Haudry, *Le feu dans la tradition indo-européenne*, Archè, Milano 2017.

year."[2] The runic inscription on the Stentoften runestone (Sweden, early 7th century), gives it the ideographic value of "prosperity, prosperous year." It's quite possible that the two elements that make the rune Il indicates the two parts of the year (or even the dual moon, ascending and descending), especially since its position is right in the middle of the *Fuþark*. "It could be," writes Wolfgang Krause, "that its shape symbolizes the two semesters of the year, if we go by a symbol with a similar shape found in numerous materials, for instance on the clay container found in Havors (Gotland), which dates to the 4th century."[3] So it seems that the rune twelve splits *fuþark* letters into two equal parts, and corresponds to some sort of equinoctial axis (the year begins at the fall equinox, so at the beginning of the dark period). The first half of the runes denotes by their acronyms some rather "varunian" aspects, meaning nocturnal and dangerous, and the other half some rather "mitrian" aspects, associated with good and light. Incidentally it is also very interesting to note that this rune is one of those which does not have an equivalent in any Mediterranean alphabet that could have inspired runic writing.[4]

---

2 In several Slavic languages, the term for year can also refer to the spring: *jaro* "spring" in Slovakian, *jaro* in Czech, *jar* in Old Polish, *jar* in Serbo-Croatian, *jara* or *jaru* in Old Russian, *jar* in Ukrainian, same meaning. See also *Jarilo* from the Belarusian folklore, who's an ancient god of the spring revival.

3 *Les runes*, op. cit., p. 51.

4 The rune ᛞ on the other hand is somewhat similar to the Chinese ideogram *tchōng*, which precisely means "middle." One could also find some connection with the symbol of the double-bitted axe.

26

Asterisms and Constellations

THE *FUÞARK* COMPRISES TWENTY-FOUR SIGNS. Those twenty-four signs are grouped into three eight-sign long sequences, but given the homology mentioned earlier in this books, the number twenty-four can also allude to the division of the day into twenty-four hours or the division of the year into twenty-four periods of fourteen nights (fortnight),[1] or even to the twelve months in a year. The ancient Indo-European cultures didn't have a base ten system, a system that became prevalent only much later on.[2] They had a duodecimal system. This brings us to another theory, which links the *Fuþark* to the zodiac constellations, and even if it is tenuous, the theory is still interesting.

The nocturnal sky is the best example of a sky map. Ever since prehistory, orientations of caves or megalithic monuments (Stonehenge, Newgrange, Goseck), as well as orientations of cave paintings (like in Pech Merle and Lascaux) have been set according to astronomical observations (sunrises and sunsets during the summer or winter solstice, or during equinoxes, etc.) A huge literature has been dedicated this day to "archaeo-astronomy," which seems to be particularly expansive for the Germanic people and the Celts. Caesar wrote that the druids had "numerous speculations about celestial bodies and their motions" (*De bello gallico*, VI, 12).

---

1 The Chinese also kept in memory the use of an ancient subdivision of the year in twenty-four *tsieki*.

2 It was not adopted in France until the Revolution, on the 5th October, 1793.

Those speculations were also, of course, about stars (from the Indo-European *ster). Uniting stars into constellations with specific names, observing the zodiac, and later on identifying four cardinal points in the horizon, as well as the moments when seasons begin, seem to have been done in Europe on a very early date, totally independently from the Mesopotamian zodiac mentioned in texts from the first millennium BC.[3] The zodiac is a circular area of the celestial sphere, whose ecliptic is centered on the middle and which comprises the twelve constellations that the sun goes through in a year. The moon and the sun never go outside this fairly narrow area. The number of zodiac parts comes from the sidereal motion of the moon, which is in retrograde for 13° 20' every day with the depth of the sky on the ecliptic as a reference.

The Indo-Aryans came up with that stellar mapping by identifying some asterisms on or near the ecliptic. An asterism is a singular figure made of particularly bright stars (Altair in the constellation of Aquila, Vega in the constellation of Lyra, the W of Cassiopeia, Orion's Sword and Orion's Belt, etc.). Different cultures came up with constellations based on asterisms. Constellations associate several stars based on perspective effects that make them stand out together. In Vedic India, they were used to count sidereal days in lunar months. The Indian lunar zodiac was first made of twenty-four and then twenty-seven "moon dwellings" (*nakṣatra*), some powers of the Night that are listed in the *Taittirīya saṃhitā* (*Yajur-Veda*) (II.13.20), the *Kāthaka saṃhitā* (39.13) and the *Atharva-Veda* (19.7). There is as many asterisms as there are days in a sidereal month (twenty-seven, thirty-two days), the moon goes from one asterism to the next every day. Every *nakṣatra* was then divided into quarters (*padas*). In the *Taittirīya Brāhmana* (i, 5, 2, 7), the twenty-seven *nākshatra* are called "houses of gods." The moon (male) is described in that system as the "king (or master) of the stars" (*nakṣatra-rāja*).

---

3   See Alexander A. Gurshtein, "Did the Pre-Indo-Europeans Influence the Formation of the Western Zodiac?," in *The Journal of Indo-European Studies*, spring-summer 2005, pp. 103–150. The author demonstrates that the former "zodiac square," where Gemini corresponded to the spring equinox, Virgo corresponded to the summer solstice, Sagittarius to the fall equinox and Pisces to the winter solstice, is linked to the Indo-European myth of the divine Twins "bringing back" in the spring the Daughter of the Sun that went missing in the winter. See also Eric P. Hamp, "The Principal (?) Indo-European Constellations," in *Proceedings of the Eleventh International Congress of Linguistics*, Il Mulino, Bologna 1974, pp. 1047–1055.

Some tried to find a connection between the twenty-seven *nākshatra* and the twenty-seven Valkyries mentioned in the Edda, and also the twenty-seven Gandharvas. Some also tried to demonstrate that the twelve "celestial dwellings" (*Himmelsburgen*) described in the *Grímnismál* (str. 4–17) were a ancient description of the Germanic zodiac (it was the opinion of Finn Magnusen and Karl Simrock). It is a possibility but it is hardly verifiable. The now famous bronze Nebra sky disk found in 1999 in ex-East Germany that dates back to 1600 BC is the oldest Germanic depiction of the sky. It is composed of a moon crescent and a full moon, thirty-two stars (including the Pleiades), two arcs of a circle and a solar barge. The Greek Pleiades correspond in India to the *Krittikā*, whose name make them "splitters" (they split the year into two parts). They are sometimes embodied by caregivers of Kārttikeya, son of Shiva.

The *Hávamál*, as we've seen earlier in this book, narrates Óðinn's discovery of the runes after he having hanged for "nine full nights" (str. 138), how he "picked up the runes" after having "looked down" (str. 139), but how was he hanging? Jere Fleck thinks that he could only have been hanging by the feet, or even by a foot (like the Hanged Man, the twelfth card in a Tarot deck), because he could only have leaned down and picked up the runes that were "down below," which would have been impossible had he been hanging from the neck.[4] This remark is not absurd. What does one see when ones hangs by the feet during the night? The sky and in particular the constellations. So, were the runes that Óðinn discovered made in the image of the constellations that he could have watched for nine full nights? Are we supposed to understand that the nights were nine consecutive nights, the span of nine "full moons" or, considering the possible homology between nights, days and years, could it even have been nine years? It is at least worthy of some consideration.

There is a theory according to which the runic signs that brought forth the *Fuþark*'s letters have an "astronomical" origin. This theory has been expressed in a number of books, of varying quality, some of them being completely whimsical.[5] However we cannot dismiss it a priori. Jean Vertemont

---

4 Jere Fleck, "Odin's Self-Sacrifice — A New Interpretation," in *Scandinavian Studies*, spring 1971, pp. 119–142, and autumn 1971, pp. 385–413.

5 Herman Wirth (*Der Aufgang der Menschheit. Untersuchungen zur Geschichte der Religion, Symbolik und Schrift der Atlantisch-Nordischen Rasse*, Diederichs, Jena 1928;

and Jean-Gabriel Foucaud write that "making the first rune, Fehu, coincides with the Pleiades, which are considered to be the first dwelling in the Vedas, makes the shapes of all the following asterisms as well as their order in the ecliptic coincide with the shapes of all the runes and their order in the Elder *Fuþark* [...] This symmetry isn't based on individual elements, it is based on a full set of elements, which makes it valid."[6] So, arranging signs into three *ættir*, which was influenced by the division of the lunar cycle into three phases, supposedly also reflects the division of the sky into three distinct sets of constellations or asterisms. The peculiar order of the *Fuþark* is then supposedly explained by being "the order given by the ancient zodiac, which is expressed by the runes in agreement with the Indian lunar zodiac of the *nakṣatra*."[7] The twenty-four runes supposedly correspond to the twelve constellations or asterisms represented by two consecutive runes for each of them, and the zodiac gives us the key to identify the ascending and descending periods of the moon. Unfortunately, there's a shortage of decisive evidence for this theory.

Nevertheless, let's keep in mind the homology between the three *ættir* of the *Fuþark* (3 x 8 letters = 24), the three phases of the Moon (3 x 8 nights = 24), the three periods of the day (3 x 8 hours = 24), the three original seasons of the year that used to be symbolized by the Hours (3 x 8 half-months = 24).

The mystery surrounding the origin of runic writing is far from being solved.

Die heilige Urschrift der Menschheit, Koehler u. Amelang, Leipzig 1931–1935) saw in the runes symbols that referred to celestial bodies or constellations as early as the Magdalenian. Some similar speculations have been suggested by Otto Sigfrid Reuter, *Germanische Himmelskunde. Untersuchungen zur Geschichte des Geistes*, op. cit., a book that is remarkably documented by the way. See also Franz Dornseiff, *Das Alphabet in Mystik und Magie*, B. G. Teubner, Leipzig 1922; Rudolf Drößler, *Als die Sterne Götter waren. Sonne, Mond und Sterne im Spiegel von Archäologie*, Kunst und Kult, Prisma, Leipzig 1976; Gert Meier, *Und das Wort ward Schrift. Von der Spracharchäologie zur Archäologie der Ideogramme. Ein Beitrag zur Entstehung des Alphabets*, Haupt, Bern 1991; Elémire Zolla, *Uscite dal mondo*, Adelphi, Milano 1992 ("Le rune e lo zodiac," pp. 145–173). One can also refer to "Sternbilder — Tierkreisbilder" du *Handwörterbuch des deutschen Aberglaubens*, vol. 9, Walter de Gruyter, Berlin 1938–41, pp. 596–690.

6 Jean Vertemont and Jean-Gabriel Foucaud, *Runes et chamanisme*, Véga, Paris 2008, p. 63. See also Jean Vertemont, "Runes et astérismes védiques," in *Antaios*, winter 1995, pp. 116–122; "Les runes et le zodiaque à 24 divisions," in *Antaios*, winter 1999, pp. 146–152.

7 Ibid., p. 157.

ILLUSTRATED STONES FROM GOTLAND (8th century) in the hall of the Sweddish History Museum.

ONE OF THE WALLS OF THE KING'S GRAVE near Kivik in Skåne, a Nordic Bronze Age sepulcher's burial mound that has been restored. It depicts ancient symbols and petroglyphs: persons, ships, war chariots, lures, etc.

THE RUNESTONE OF THE SWEDISH KING Eric the Victorious from Haddeby (Haithabu), dating to the 8th century.

THE FAMOUS AUZON CASKET (Haute-Loire) was made in the 7th century in northern England. Runes are engraved in its slabs of whalebone. One of its sides depicts an episode of the legend of Wayland the Smith, and a scene evoking worshipping mages. Nowadays, it resides in the British Museum. This chest is also known as the "Franks Casket," from the name of Sir Wollaston Franks who acquired it in 1857.

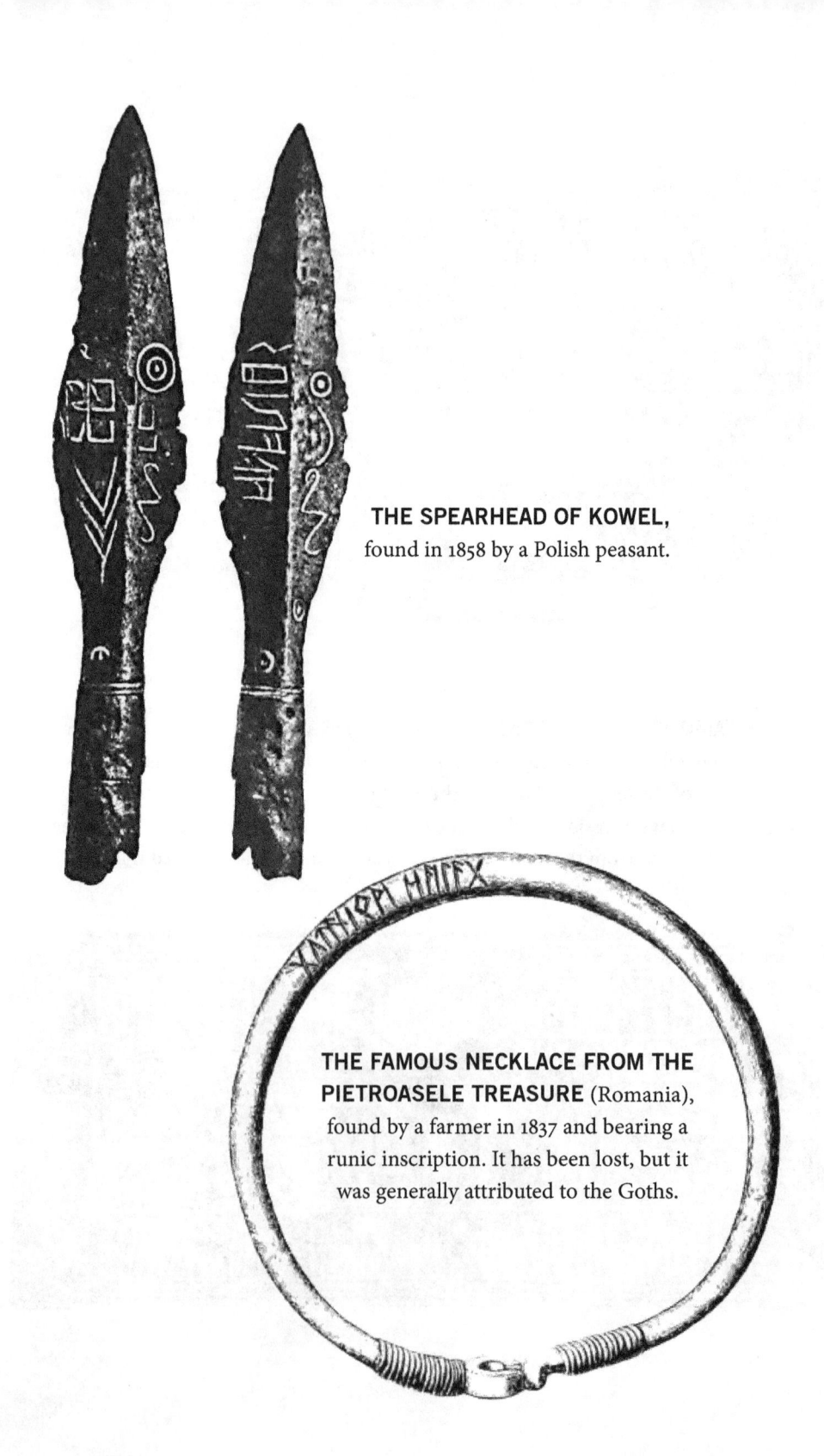

THE SPEARHEAD OF KOWEL,
found in 1858 by a Polish peasant.

THE FAMOUS NECKLACE FROM THE PIETROASELE TREASURE (Romania), found by a farmer in 1837 and bearing a runic inscription. It has been lost, but it was generally attributed to the Goths.

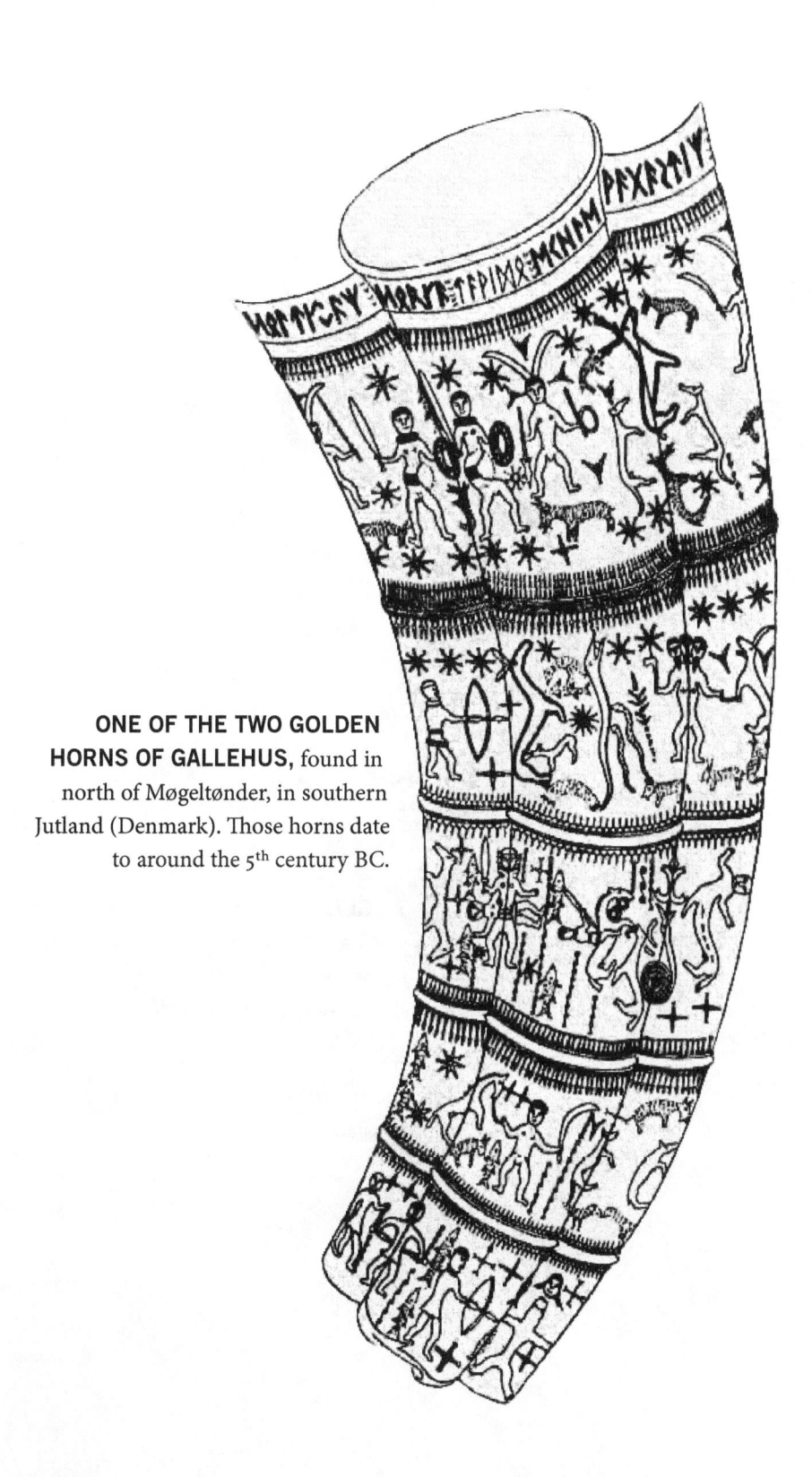

ONE OF THE TWO GOLDEN HORNS OF GALLEHUS, found in north of Møgeltønder, in southern Jutland (Denmark). Those horns date to around the 5th century BC.

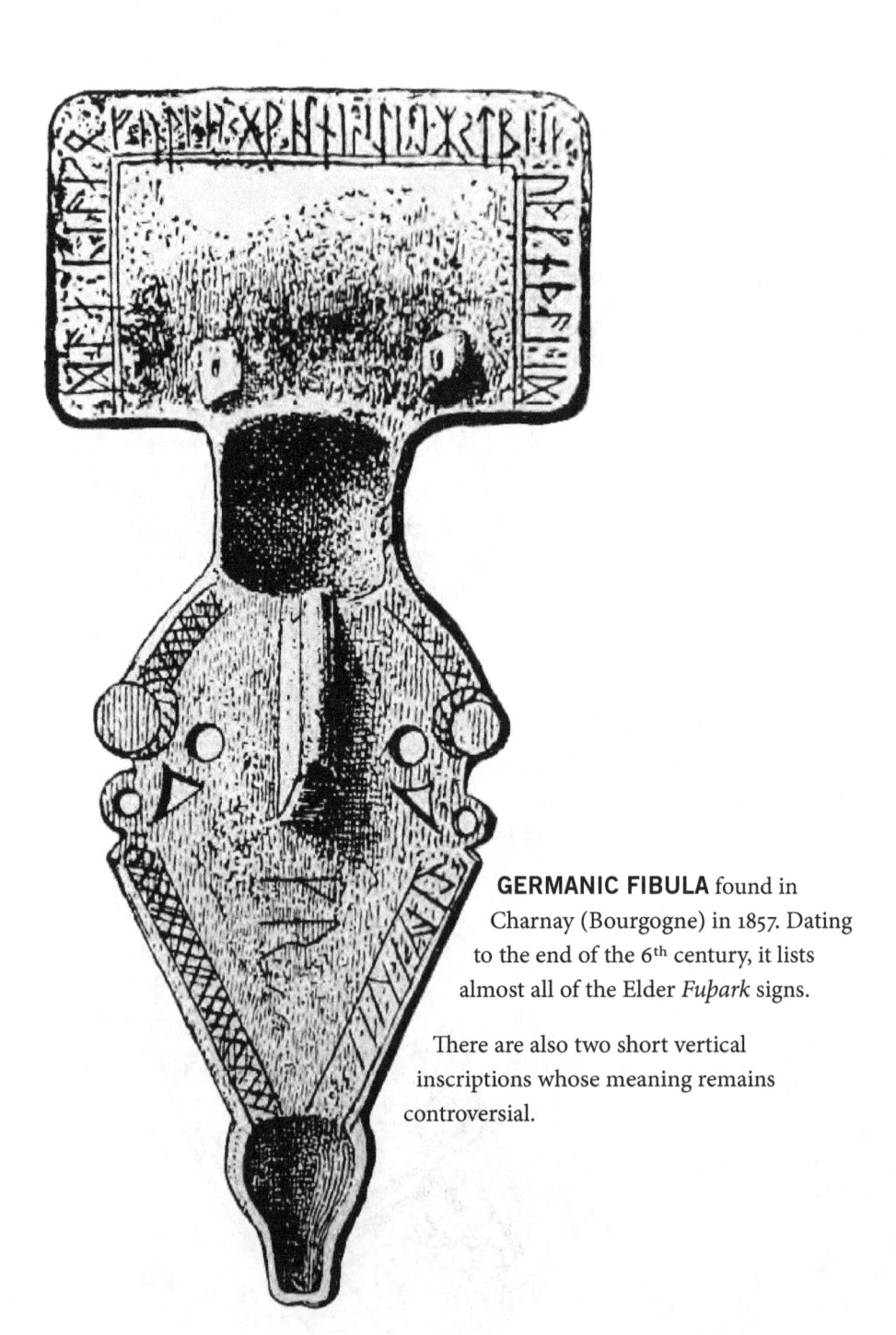

GERMANIC FIBULA found in Charnay (Bourgogne) in 1857. Dating to the end of the 6th century, it lists almost all of the Elder *Fuþark* signs.

There are also two short vertical inscriptions whose meaning remains controversial.

"STICKS USED TO KNOW TIME." Illustration from *A Description of the Northern Peoples* by Olaus Magnus (Rome, 1555). This book was the principal reference regarding Scandinavian countries in the second half of the 16th century.

PART IV

27

"Phoinika Grammata"

HERODOTUS, WHO WROTE ABOUT the story of Cadmus (whose name seems to have come from *kekadmai* in Greek) in the 5th century BC. Cadmus was the son of the king of Tyre named Agenor and of Telephassa, who came to Greek looking for her sister Europa, who was abducted by Zeus in the form of a bull.[1] Europa had three sons fathered by Zeus: Minos, Rhadamanthus, and Sarpedon. Cadmus, who was from Phoenicia, allegedly founded the city of Thebes and spread there the alphabet, "that was until then unknown to the Hellenes, to my knowledge." This is the reason why the Greeks called the letters of their alphabet *phoinika grammata*, "Phoenician letters."

Herodotus didn't write that the Phoenicians invented the alphabet, as it is often believed. He just wrote that they brought it to Greece: "When settling in the country, the Phoenicians who came with Cadmus brought to the Greeks a lot of knowledge, among others, the alphabet." Tacitus also wrote that "the Egyptians call themselves the inventors of writing and claim that it spread from them to Greece with the help of Phoenicians, because they were the masters of the sea. They took credit for inventing something they were taught" (*Annals*, XI, 14). Diodorus Siculus was just as cautious because he

---

1 Herodotus, *Histories*, V, 57–59. On the abduction of Europa, see Ovid, *Metamorphoses*, II, 839 ff. The Greek legend states that Agenor was the son of Poseidon, that he settled down in Phoenicia and had three sons: Phoenix, who stayed in Phoenicia, Cilix, who conquered the southern coast of Anatolia, and Cadmus, who settled down in Greece.

only mentioned two traditions, none citing the Phoenicians as the inventors of the alphabet. According to the first tradition, the Phoenicians learned the letters of the alphabet from "Syrians," and then shared that knowledge after having tweaked the shapes of some of them. According to the second tradition, Orpheus discovered writing by being taught by the Muses, and then spread to Greece "from the North."[2] It should be noted that according to the Greeks, Orpheus also invented magic.

---

2   Diodorus Siculus, III, 67 and V, 74. See also Marcel Detienne, *L'écriture d'Orphée*, Gallimard, Paris 1989, pp. 101–115.

28

From the Phoenicians to the Greeks

BESIDE THE FORMAL RESEMBLANCE between the two writing systems, the theory of Phoenician origin for the Greek alphabet seems to be confirmed by the fact that the Greeks kept designating their letters (*alpha, bēta,* derived from *'aleph, beth,* etc.) in a meaningless way from their language's perspective. The order of the Greek and Phoenician letters is also fundamentally the same. But specialists are divided on the issue of the location, date and circumstances where the Phoenician spread their writing to the Greeks.[1]

It was reckoned for a long time that the borrowing of Phoenician writing by the Greeks took place at a fairly late date, because the oldest alphabetical inscriptions that we know of (generally written from right to left or in boustrophedon mode) were dated to around 700 BC. The inscriptions in question are the texts found on the island of Thera, the Dipylon inscription, Nestor's cup from Pithecusses, on the island of Ischia, some shards

---

1   See Verein zur Förderung der Aufarbeitung der Hellenischen Geschichte e.V. (ed.), *Die Geschichte der hellenischen Sprache und Schrift, vom 2. zum 1. Jahrtausend v.Chr.: Bruch oder Kontinuität?*, Kultur und Wissenchaft, Altenburg 1998, notamment les communications de Rudolf Wachter ("Die Übernahme des Alphabets durch die Griechen: wie, wann, wo, durch wen und wozu? Eine aktuelle Abwägung der Standpunkte, Argumente und methodischen Ansätze," pp. 345–353) and Wolfgang Röllig ("Das Alphabet und sein Weg zu den Griechen," pp. 359–384).

from Corinth, vases from Hymettus. It was also Rhys Carpenter's opinion, who did not think that Greek writing went further back than 720–700 BC.[2] But since then, the number of archaic Greek inscriptions has grown. The oldest ones, of the Euboean kind (the Euboans spoke an Ionian dialect), date to 770–750, if not earlier. One of the most important discoveries was an inscription in the Euboean Greek alphabet on a vase from around 750 BC found in 1984 in Italy, in the Osteria dell'Osa necropolis, in Lazio. This discovery shows that even before the Greek colonization of the Italian peninsula, the Euboean alphabet had spread to that region. Another alphabetical Greek inscription dating to −740 was found in 2001 on the bronze bowl in Midas's burial mound in Gordium (Gordion), capital of ancient Phrygia. "The available data," writes Maria Giulia Amadasi Guzzo, "confirms that the Greeks knew how to write as early as the first quarter of the 8th century and that the first one to use 'Phoenician letters' were the Euboeans."[3] Moreover, the very existence of a list of the winners of the Olympic games, which started in 776 BC, gives us reason to believe that there was a writing at the time. John F. Healey writes:

> The diversification of Greek writings took some time, which suggests that the date when the alphabet was imported is much earlier than the 8th century [...] Furthermore, in the 8th century, writing from right to left was already the norm for writings derived from Phoenician, so it is hard to imagine the Greeks borrowing the alphabet at such a late date and showing hesitations on what the writing direction should be.[4]

Nowadays, the Greek alphabet is commonly believed to have appeared from the end of the 10th century BC to the beginning of the 9th century BC, if not earlier. Margherita Guarducci believes it was in the 9th century.[5] John F. Healey thinks that "the earliest possible date would likely be around 1100–1050," which matches Berthold Louis Ullmann's 1930s estimations

---

2   Rhys Carpenter, "The Antiquity of the Greek Alphabet," in *American Journal of Archaeology*, 1933, pp. 8–29.

3   Maria Giulia Amadasi Guzzo, "La transmission de l'alphabet phénicien aux Grecs," in Rina Viers (ed.), Des *signes pictographiques à l'alphabet. La communication écrite en Méditerranée*, Karthala, Paris 2000, p. 235.

4   John F. Healey, *Les débuts de l'alphabet*, 2nd ed., Seuil, Paris 2005, p. 61.

5   Margherita Guarducci, *Epigrafia greca*, Istituto poligrafico dello Stato, Roma 1967.

that put the borrowing in the 11th or 12th century BC, meaning during the Dorian invasions.[6] "It seems plausible," writes Charles Higounet, "that the borrowing and adaptation of the Phoenician alphabet by the Greeks took place around the end of the 2nd millennium, or at the very beginning of the 1st one."[7]

The location where the transmission took place is just as much talked about. Many diverse theories have been put forth (Cyprus, Rhodes, Crete, Asia minor, etc.), but they are only suppositions. The fact that there were originally several different Greek alphabets hinders theories arguing that there was a unique source.[8] The unification of those alphabets took place during the writing reform in Athens in 403–402, which made the Ionic alphabet the standard.

Unlike what some thought, the Greeks definitely did not start using writing for economic or trading purposes -bookkeeping-, because no economic document has been found in the Greek world during the beginnings of writing. The initial use of writing seems to have rather been linked with poetic notation, especially in the case of Homeric poems. There is no doubt that the formatting of the Iliad and the Odyssey as we know them is linked to the use of alphabetical writing in Greece.[9]

Still, the question of the Phoenician alphabet's transmission to Greece remains open. How could Phoenician writing give birth to Greek writing?

---

6   Berthold Louis Ullmann, *Ancient Writing and its Influence*, Longmans Green & Co., New York 1932. "One can't help but put side by side the adoption of Phoenician writing at the time and the fact that the Dorian invasion seems to have been at least partially by sea. The Dorians went from the south to the north in the Peloponnese, and it is plausible that they occupied Crete before that," wrote James Février ("La genèse de l'alphabet," in *Revue des cours et conférences*, 30 March 1939, p. 718).

7   Charles Higounet, *L'écriture*, 5th ed., PUF, Paris 1976, p. 60.

8   See Lilian Hamilton Jeffery, *The Local Scripts of Archaic Greece. A Study of the Origin of the Greek Alphabet and its Development from the Eigth to the Fifth Centuries B.C.*, Clarendon Press, Oxford 1961.

9   Barry B. Powell (*Homer and the Origin of Greek Alphabet*, Cambridge University Press, Cambridge 1991) goes as far as saying the Greek alphabet was introduced specifically to note the Homeric poems. The writing is mentioned only once by Homer, in the passage of the *Iliad* (that we already cited) where the king of Argos Prœtos gives Bellerophon a message to deliver to the king of Lycia. The fact that there is only one mention shouldn't come as a surprise if, as it is likely to be the case, Homeric poems come from a long oral tradition.

Was there a borrowing or did both the Phoenicians and the Greeks use at the same an alphabet derived from a common set of signs?[10] Can the similarity between the two writings be explained by causation, a common heritage, or both?

An alphabetical writing implies the complete breakdown of the language's sounds into simple phonemes. The twenty-two letter Phoenician alphabet isn't actually one since it doesn't include the vowels. Its signs are associated with a full syllable made of a constant consonant and a variable vowel. But a consonantal writing didn't suit the notation of a language like Greek, which indicates the function of a word in a sentence by adding a ending most of the time made of a vowel. James Février goes as far as writing that in his opinion, "there was no reason for the Greeks to adopt Phoenician writing."[11]

As a full-fledged alphabet, as early as the 8th century the Greek alphabet was made of twenty-four signs, vowels and consonants. The Greeks introduced vowels, maybe because they wanted to keep "the memory of the former Mycenaean syllabary, which made a clear cut between syllables from different sets of vowels," writes François Chamoux.[12] The vowels were supposedly obtained from the conversion of some guttural Phoenician consonants (the consonant *'alef* became the vowel *alpha*, *hé* became *epsilon*, *wau* gave birth to *digamma* and then to *upsilon*, *yod* was converted into *iota*, *ayin* into *omicron*). Adding those vowels, which were called in the Middle Ages *Matres lectionis*, "mothers of reading," has obviously been decisive. The first beneficiaries were literature and poetry, and then tragedy.[13] Indeed, it is only then that the writing system could represent all the sounds of the language, with a single character for each phoneme. The number of characters was

---

10 Let us note a curious fact here, a fact that is hard to draw conclusions from. In the Phoenician alphabet, the *first* letter, *'aleph*, the ancestor of our "A," comes from the stylized representation of a bovine head. In the *Fuþark*, the first runic letter, F, which is called *fehu* (*faihu* in the Gothic alphabet, **fehu* being its reconstructed form for Proto-Germanic from that correspondence and *fehu* in Old Saxon), has the well-established symbolic meaning of "cattle, wealth," but here it's most likely sheep.

11 James Février, art. cit., p. 719.

12 François Chamoux, *La civilisation grecque*, Arthaud, Paris 1963, p. 55.

13 It should be noted that Homer's *Odyssey* begins by a vowel: *Ándra moi énnette, Moûsa, polútropon, ós mála pollá*, "Tell me, Muse, that subtle man who wandered for so long."

also limited. Whereas the former syllabaries make a symbol match with sound for every individual sound of the language, which can end in systems made up of hundreds of signs, the Greek alphabet breaks down the syllable into all its phonic parts. It abandons the syllable as a graphic unit ("ba be bi bo bu," etc.) and substitutes it for a very different kind of unit, a more abstract king ("a b c d e," etc.) that goes against the most immediate perception of language. That is why Eric A. Havelock said that the Greek system can be considered to be "the first and only genuine alphabet."[14]

---

14 Eric A. Havelock, *Aux origines de la civilisation écrite en Occident*, François Maspéro, Paris 1981, p. 36. Ignace Jay Gelb (*Pour une théorie de l'écriture*, Flammarion, Paris 1973) went as far as questioning whether the systems that don't include vowels should be considered to be true alphabets: According to him, consonantal alphabets should rather be considered to be syllabaries in which every sign represents a consonant followed by a vowel.

29

Before the Phoenicians

THERE WERE MANY WRITING systems present in the Eastern Mediterranean and the Near East much before the Phoenicians. The two oldest ones, which are also the most famous and well-spread ones, are the Egyptian hieroglyphs and the Sumerian cuneiform writing. Both seem to have appeared in the middle of the 4th millennium BC. The first Egyptian hieroglyphs appeared around −3400, under the dynasty of Thinis, so before the birth of the proper pharaonic civilization. The most ancient known artefact is the tablets of Ahā, the first king of the dynasty of Thinis. The hieroglyphic writing was the one used on monuments, which was later on simplified into hieratic writing and then into demotic writing. However, the first great discursive texts with complex sentences only appear around −2680, under Djoser's (or Djeser) reign, sovereign of the third dynasty, who built the pyramid in Saqqara.

The Sumerian tradition attributes the invention of writing to Enmerkar, the second representative of the Uruk dynasty. The most ancient known artefact bearing writing, clay tablets called Uruk IV with archaic cuneiform signs, supposedly date back to 3200 BC, but that date was not confirmed. The origin of the Sumerians, a people who were neither Indo-European nor Semitic — which is also the case for the Elamites, the Hurrians and the Urartians — remains mysterious. Their ethnogenesis was first thought to have been central Asia, but the theory was dropped. In 1951, the American assyriologist Ephraim Avigdor Speiser thought that they settled in

Lower-Mesopotamia, probably by the sea from a site located to the east. In France, André Parrot leaned towards Anatolia and so believed they came from the north. The Sumerian civilization actually could have been the result of a pre-Indo-European wave of expansion that eventually became the Mediterranean cultures that used to be commonly called "Asianic," because they weren't Semitic nor Indo-European.

Like the other peoples related to them, the Sumerians spoke an agglutinating language, meaning (in opposition to inflected languages) a language that adds pre- or post-posited particles to verbal or nominal roots that are generally invariable. Cuneiform writing, that quickly started being called Sumero-Akkadian, was also used all over Asia minor, mainly for utilitarian purposes.

The "Proto-Sinaitic" script should also be mentioned. This term refers to about thirty inscriptions found in 1904 by the Englishman Flinders Petrie near the mining camps of Serabit el-Khadim in the desert of the Sinai. The oldest ones are graffitis that supposedly go back to around 1600 BC. Alan Gardiner offered in 1916 a deciphering that still isn't unanimously supported. These inscriptions comprise some sort of alphabet seemingly derived from Egyptian hieroglyphs which seems to denote a west Semitic language. Gerhard Herm attributes them to "'Canaanites,' meaning Proto-Phoenicians from the libano-palestinian region."[1] They were also attributed to the Hyksos,[2] a population whose origin is very poorly known.

The Hyksos (in Egyptian demotic *heka khasewet*, literally "masters of foreign lands") are said to have introduced the war chariot to Egypt, as well as the composite bow and weapons birthed from the bronze industry. A west Semitic origin was sometimes attributed to them, but recent works have shown that their language does not belong to the Semitic language group.[3] They invaded Egypt, where they removed the leaders of the fourteenth dynasty and founded the fifteenth and sixteenth dynasties (between 1674 and 1548 BC). In 1933, Carl Watzinger was the first to give them a Hurrian

---

1 Gerhard Herm, *Les Phéniciens. L'antique royaume de la pourpre*, Fayard, Paris 1976, p. 223.

2 See André Lemaire, "Les 'Hyksos' and les débuts de l'écriture alphabé- tique au Proche-Orient," in Rina Viers (ed.), *Des signes pictographiques à l'alphabet*, op. cit., pp. 103–133.

3 See Dominique Valbelle, "Hyksos," in Jean Leclant (ed.), *Dictionnaire de l'Antiquité*, PUF, Paris 2005, p. 1106.

origin. His theory was then picked up by the German Egyptologist Hans Wolfgang Helck, who saw in them a composite blend of Hurrians and Indo-Europeans that migrated east to first settle in Anatolia.[4] Gerharm Herm considers them to be "Indo-Germanic." But they were also suggested to have been Amorites, form Akkadians, Syro-Canaanites, Proto-Phoenicians and even Mycenaeans. The very reality of a Hyksos invasion was also questioned by some authors, in particular Jürgen von Beckerath.[5]

Finally, there are the Cretan writings, among which the most famous is Linear A. Its vestiges were discovered by Arthur Evans at the beginning of the 20th century.[6] This writing, which has yet to be deciphered, was used in ancient Crete during the period of the first Minoan palaces, so around 1900 BC. Distinct from the ancient Cretan hieroglyphic, Linear A comprised eighty-five signs and ideograms. Its older inscriptions are on clay tablets found in the Hagia Triada archaeological site in southern Crete. Harald Haarmann[7] suggested that the writing was brought by populations who came from Danubian cultures of the "Old Europe," and that they were chased out by the arrival of Indo-Europeans to the Aegean Sea, Crete and the Cyclades. There was also the theory that Linear A didn't represent an agglutinating language, like it was believed for a long time, but rather a language related

---

4   Hans Wolfgang Helck, *Die Beziehungen Ägyptens zu Vorderasien im 3. und 2. Jahrtausend v. Chr.*, Otto Harrassowitz, Wiesbaden 1962.

5   Jürgen von Beckerath, *Chronologie des pharaonischen Ägypten. Die Zeitbestimmung der ägyptischen Geschichte von der Vorzeit bis 332 v. Chr.*, Philipp von Zabern, Mainz 1997. On this issue, see John Van Seter, *The Hyksos. A New Investigation*, Yale University Press, New Haven 1966; Donald Bruce Redford, "The Hyksos Invasion in History and Tradition," in *Orientalia*, 1970, pp. 1–51.

6   See Arthur Evans, *Scripta Minoa, the Written Documents of Minoan Crete. With Special Reference to the Archive of Knossos*, Clarendon Press, Oxford 1909; William C. Brice, *Inscriptions in the Minoan Linear Script of Class A*, Oxford University Press, Oxford 1961.

7   Harald Haarmann, "Writing from Old Europe to Ancient Crete. A Case of Cultural Continuity," in *The Journal of Indo-European Studies*, autumn-winter 1989, pp. 251–275. See also Wilhelm Hauer, *Schrift der Götter. Vom Ursprung der Runen*, Orion-Heimreiter, Kiel 2006; Hans-Günter Buchholz, "Die ägäischen Schriftsysteme und ihre Ausstrahlung in die ostmediterranen Kulturen," in Dietrich Gerhardt (ed.), *Frühe Schriftzeugnisse der Menschheit*, Vandenhoeck u. Ruprecht, Göttingen 1969, pp. 88–150.

to Luwian (or Luvian) or another language from the Anatolian group, or even the Indo-Iranian branch of Indo-European.[8]

Linear A, which was a tool of the Minoan thalassocracy, spread far and wide on the continent and all over the Aegean basin as from the middle of the 15th century BC: it was found in Cyprus, in most of the Aegaen Sea islands, and as far as the Aeolian Islands, north of Sicily. From that writing sprung other writings, like the Cyprio-Minoan (around the 16th century BC), the Linear B (around the 15th century BC), and the syllabic Cypriot (not before the 11th century BC). The destruction of the Minoan civilization by the Mycenaeans brought about its disappearance, except maybe in Cyprus.

Linear B appeared in Create around 1400–1350 BC. We know from the deciphering conducted in the 1950s by Michael Ventris and John Chadwick that it represented a primitive Greek dialect. The older continental inscriptions (Pylos, Mycenae, Thebes, etc.) date to slightly more than a century later. It disappeared with the collapse of the Mycenaean empire.

---

8   See Hubert La Marle, *Linéaire A: la première écriture syllabique de Crète*, 4 vol., Geuthner, Paris 1997–1999; *Introduction au linéaire A. Lire et comprendre l'écriture syllabique de Crète minoenne*, Geuthner, Paris 2000.

30

The Phoenician Alphabet

A "CANAANITE" ALPHABET anterior to 1200 BC was found in 1948 in the Ugarit archeological site, in northern Syria (now Ras Shamra). It is a consonantal alphabet, but it uses cuneiform signs. So, it is completely different from the Phoenician alphabet's letters, and it didn't grow into anything more than that. Phoenician writing appeared at an unknown date, but it is certain that it was before the 11th century BC. Indeed, around 1000 BC, all the consonants are already in place in this twenty-two-sign alphabet. Françoise Briquel-Chatonnet points out that the order of the letters "is almost contemporary of the appearance of the alphabet."[1] The famous inscription found in 1923 by Pierre Montet, the inscription engraved in the name of the king Ithobaal of Byblos (currently Jbail, north of Beiruth) on two sides of king Ahiram's sarcophagus, dates to around 1050 BC. This inscription reads from right to left. Its dating is not entirely confirmed (another dating making it older has been suggested). Some other, shorter texts that could go as far back as the 13th and 12th centuries BC have also been found on the Syrian coast, in particular on arrowheads.

We don't really know where the Phoenician alphabet was born. Some say Byblos, but Palestine is where the most inscriptions in 2nd millennium

---

1   Françoise Briquel-Chatonnet, "Naissance de l'alphabet," in L'Histoire, June 1992, p. 21. See also Wolfgang Röllig, "Das phönizische Alphabet und die frühen europäischen Schriften," in *Die Phönizier im Zeitalter Homers*, Philipp von Zabern, Mainz 1990, pp. 87–95.

BC alphabetical writing have been found. This writing flourished significantly in the five former kingdoms of the Philistine plain: Gaza, Ashkalon, Ashdod, Gath and Ekron. Then in the kingdoms of Tyre, Sidon, Arwad and Byblos, located north of the Mount Carmel, on the Mediterranean coast of the Levant. Phoenician writing then spread to all the Phoenicians colonies and trading posts, including small kingdoms following the Luwian tradition from Asia minor. "The fact that a population, whose usual Indo-European language was the Luwian, used the Phoenician language has probably helped to spread and adapt the Phoenician alphabet to the Greek world," reckons André Lemaire.[2]

Some people attempted to make the Phoenician writing derive from the Proto-Sinaitic writing through the intermediary of Proto-Canaanite and the Ugaritic alphabets (Maurice Dunand's theory). Some people attempted to link it to the twenty-four "monoliteral" signs invented by the Egyptians, to which the Phoenicians supposedly attributed new phonetic values. Some people also tried to account for this writing by a simple desire to "simplify" the Sumero-Akkadian cuneiform writing or the Egyptian hieroglyphic writing. All these theories that are actually only suppositions and hardly convince anyone. On the Ugaritic alphabet, Maurice Vieyra wrote that the question at hand is to know whether it

> was used as a model for the Phoenician alphabet or whether both [...] represented the completion of a more ancient traditional order that was adopted by both alphabets. [But] none of the Ras Shamra alphabet's signs derives directly or indirectly from Mesopotamian cuneiform signs, not even from marginal cuneiform syllabaries [...] So it is a proper invention, not only when it comes to the creation of an alphabet, but also in the shape of the signs used by this alphabet [...] This doesn't bode well for the validity of an argument often used to try to derive the signs of Proto-Sinaitic from some Egyptians hieroglyphs.[3]

The same author underlines that "going from 'Proto-Sinaitic' signs to the letters of the Canaanite linear alphabet isn't as easy as it seems," especially since it "is definitely not clear historically or linguistically how the discovery

---

2 André Lemaire, "Origine de l'alphabet et écritures ouest-sémitiques," in Anne-Marie Christin (ed.), *Histoire de l'écriture*, op. cit., p. 213.

3 Maurice Vieyra, "Aux origines de l'alphabet," in *Atomes*, March 1966, pp. 112, 114.

would have spread from Sinai peninsula to Syria."[4] As for a desire to "simplify" the system of hieroglyphs or cuneiform signs, it seems dubious, especially since most of those signs have "no likeness with the corresponding Phoenician letters."[5]

It actually seems impossible to demonstrate that the Phoenician alphabet is derived from the Sumero-Akkadian writing, the Egyptian hieroglyphs, hieratic writing or the Proto-Sinaitic inscriptions, or that it results from an effort to "simplify" an earlier system. Marcel Cohen writes that

> the circumstances and the specific location (somewhere on the eastern coast of the Mediterranean) in which the alphabet was formed elude us. It most likely has a pictographic origin like the other writings. But we could not link it to some specific hieroglyphic documents from the Phoenician region; we aren't certain that they were connected to some engraved documents found in the Sinai, from a suspicious date (between 1800 and 1500 BC), that comprised just a few signs that looked more or less like coarse drawings.[6]

"The linear aspect of the Phoenician alphabet's letters is quite problematic," observes Maurice Vieyra:

> because it doesn't look like its shapes were naturally derived from known systems. Neither the cursive forms of the Egyptian hieroglyphs nor the 'Proto-Sinaitic' writing, which are generally considered to be its prototypes, immediately summarize the drawings that the Phoenician alphabet presents.[7]

Charles Higounet writes:

> the purpose of all the theories was to discover the origin of the material form of the Phoenician letters. At first, people tried to directly connect those forms to the forms of simple Egyptian hieroglyphs or the forms of hieratic signs. Some other scholars thought those forms were a deformation of the cuneiform characters [...] the linear Cretan antecedent was also brought up [...] bringing it together with the Proto-Sinaitic writing and with the Arabic writings didn't help because it seems that they are derived or parallel systems, not

---

4 Maurice Vieyra, "L'alphabet en Grèce: mythes et réalités," in *Atomes*, May 1966, p. 241.
5 James Février, "La genèse de l'alphabet," art. cit., p. 708.
6 Marcel Cohen, *Le Courrier de l'Unesco*, March 1964.
7 "L'alphabet en Grèce: mythes et réalités," art. cit., p. 240.

antecedents [...] Finally, a last group of people argued that the Phoenician characters were made from the ground up.[8]

Françoise Briquel-Chatonnet brings the topic of the appearance of the alphabetical system to a close: "we must admit that it is impossible to track the historical process that resulted in the creation of this new system, or to locate the creation with precision."[9]

So, the question that should then be asked is where do the letters of the Phoenician alphabet come from? Where did the Phoenicians find them? Who transmitted the letters to them?

---

8   *L'écriture*, op. cit., p. 44.

9   Françoise Briquel-Chatonnet, "Phénicie. Les mystères du premier alphabet," in *Comment est née l'écriture*, n° hors-série de Science et vie, June 2002, p. 60.

31

The Sea Peoples

THE TURN OF THE 12th century BC is not just a turning point but a dramatic shift in the history of the Eastern Mediterranean and the Near East. In the span of a few decades, at the end of the 13th and the beginning of the 12th century BC, the invasion of the Sea Peoples disrupted the whole Mediterranean Sea. Both the Mycenaean in Greece and the Hittite empire in Anatolia collapsed one after the other. Meanwhile, most principalities in the Levant and almost all the Bronze Age cultures of Cyprus ad the Syro-Palestinian coast were disrupted. The only territories that weathered the storm were far from the sea, like Upper Egypt and Mesopotamia.

It was a massive invasion, a true migration of peoples that's reminiscent of the "great invasions" (*Völkerwanderung*) of the High Middle Ages. It was not only raiding parties, but whole peoples with their women and children transported on the back of heavy ox-wagons who threw themselves into the conquest of a new home. This explains why the invasion of the Sea Peoples has been described as "the largest and fasted invasion that world has ever seen."[1]

Together with their Libyan, Tyrrhenian and Anatolian tribesmen allies that they carried with them along the way, the Sea peoples attacked Egypt in the Ramesses III period, who likely reigned between 1186 and 1154 BC.

---

1 Jean-Jacques Prado, *L'invasion de la Méditerranée par les peuples de l'Océan, XIIIe siècle avant Jésus-Christ*, L'Harmattan, Paris 1992.

But this time, they had some serious setbacks. The Pharaoh's troops stopped them twice and then definitively wiped out their navy at the entrance of a tributary of the Nile. This exploit that happened in 1177 BC[2] is confirmed by the cross-checking of the Harris Papyrus and what is written on the walls of the funeral temple of Medinet Habu. The Egyptian texts mention the capture of 100,000 prisoners by Ramesses III's troops.

The bas-reliefs of Medinet Haby describe with some degree of precision the attackers. They make them out to be tall, with a straight nose, often tattooed, but clean shaven and not circumcised. They are dressed in some nature of kilts and leather corselets, they are equipped with large round shields, spears and long swords (but never bows or arrows), and feathery toques (maybe eagle feathers) or helmets with tufts and chinstraps festooned with a pair of horns separated by a disk. On the ground, they used war chariots, but on the sea, they used ships whose bows and sterns were shaped as animal heads, most commonly bird heads. Moreover, they used iron metallurgy.[3]

The question of the identity and origin of the Sea Peoples remains one of the more discussed topics of the research being undertaken. Eliezer D. Oren sees it as "one of the most curiously irritating phenomenon of the history of the Mediterranean Basin."[4] Many authors confine themselves to linking them to the Aegean world, but it is hardly believable that the

---

2   According to some authors, Ramesses III actually reigned between roughly 1200 and 1168 BC. In that case, the great confrontation with the Sea Peoples should have taken place in 1190, and the first clashes should have taken place eight years earlier.

3   See Alessandra Nibbi, *The Sea Peoples and Egypt*, Noyes Press, Park Ridge 1975; Günther Hölbl, "Die historischen Aussagen der ägyptischen Seevölkerinschriften," in Sigrid Deger-Jalkotzy (ed.), *Griechenland, die Ägäis und die Levante während der "Dark Ages" vom 12. bis zum 9. Jh. v. Chr.*, Verlag der Österreichischen Akademie der Wissenschaften, Wien 1983, pp. 121–143; Gustav Adolf Lehmann, "Zum Auftreten von 'Seevölker'—Gruppen im östlichen Mittelmeerraum—eine Zwischenbilanz," ibid., pp. 79–97; Trude Dothan, "Some Aspects of the Appearance of the Sea Peoples and Philistines in Canaan," ibid., pp. 99–120; David O'Connor, "The Sea Peoples and the Egyptian Source," in Eliezer D. Oren (ed.), *The Sea Peoples and their World: A Reassessment*, University of Pennsylvania, Philadelphia 2000, pp. 85–101.

4   Eliezer D. Oren (ed.), *The Sea Peoples and their World*, op. cit., p. XVII. See also Nancy K. Sandars, *The Sea Peoples, Warriors of the Ancient Mediterranean, 1250–1150 BC*, Thames & Hudson, London 1978 (french translation: *Les Peuples de la Mer, guerriers de la Méditerranée antique*, France-Empire, Paris 1981).

population of Cyprus and Crete on its own disintegrated the whole Bronze Age Mediterranean civilization. Cyprus and Crete were more likely just a step of their expansion. Some other authors believe that they come from the Balkans and the Danube, more specifically Dalmatia or Illyria, or even southern Russia and further. It is supposedly only in a second phase that they settled somewhere in the Aegean Sea and Anatolia, where they supposedly mingled with the locals.

Egyptian texts describe the Sea Peoples as coming from "islands and land bathed by the Very-Green," "islands from the middle of the sea," "islands and continents from the global sea located all the way up north," the extremity of the "great circular ocean," the "edges of the global darkness, the end of the Earth and the columns of the sky." The Harris Papyrus also call them "peoples from the ninth arc" (the Egyptians divided the known terrestrial world into nine "arcs"). This "ninth arc" corresponds to the territories located between the 52th and 57th parallels north, so northern Germany and southern Scandinavia, or the between the 48th and 54th parallels north. Their invasions were supposedly the result of terrible natural disasters and climate change that affected their homeland. Pierre Grandet writes that "they actually belonged to one of the great Indo-European waves that left marks all over the coasts of the Mediterranean, from Sardinia to Sicily." This "Indo-European wave coming from the North supposedly mixed with Mycenaeans from the Peloponnese, and then spread to the islands and coasts of the Aegean Sea."[5] So the Sea Peoples supposedly formed a vast "multinational" coalition that way, amalgamating peoples from continental Europe and the Mediterranean who were already settled in Anatolia and the Aegean Islands.

Fred C. Woudhuizen attributes to the Sea Peoples a language related to Luwian, like the languages of the Danunians, Cilicians, Isaurians, Lydians, Kaunians, Lycians and maybe also the Carians.[6] This language is also supposedly the language of the famous Phaistos Disk. Found in 1908 in the ruins of a small Minoan palace, this disk with a roughly 15 cm diameter bears 242 pictograms on its two sides. Those pictograms are laid out on

---

5   Pierre Grandet, "La migration des Peuples de la Mer," in *L'Histoire*, April 1990, pp. 16, 19.

6   Fred C. Woudhuizen, *The Language of the Sea Peoples*, Najade Press, Amsterdam 1992.

a spiral delineated by bars that make sixty-one boxes. There are forty-five signs present on it and, apparently, they could be read outwards from the center of the disk. They supposedly have nothing in common with Cretan hieroglyphs or Linear A, which kills any hope of linking them to the Minoan iconographic directory. It seems that one of the signs represent a warrior's head wearing a plumed helmet just like the haircut attributed to the Sea Peoples described on the walls of the temple of Medinet Haby. Vladimir Georgiev has also connected the Phaistos Disk to the Luwian language,[7] and Jean Faucounau linked it to some ancient Proto-Ionian.[8]

Egyptian sources also mention the names of the Sea Peoples and name the ten most important tribes: the Eqwesh, the Denyens, the Derden, the Lukkas, the Peleset, the Shekelesh maybe from the region of Sagalassos in Anatolia, the Sherden maybe from the Balkans, the Teresh, the Tjeker, and finally the Weshesh maybe from Ionia.

After their defeat to Ramesses III's troops, all these peoples went back to Cyprus and the coasts of the Levant, before scattering all over the Mediterranean. It is very likely that the Sardis and the Sicels sprung out of the Sherden and the Shekelesh, and they gave their names to Sardinia and Sicily. The Peleset became the Philistines and settled in Palestine. The Teresh settled in Troad and were most probably the ancestors of the Tyrrhenians and the Etruscans. The Eqwesh were the ancestors of the Achaeans, and the Derden were probably identical to the Dardanoi mentioned by Homer in the *Iliad*. The Denyen supposedly settled in Galilee, and the Lukkas supposedly became the Lycians.

---

7 Vladimir Georgiev, "Le déchiffrement du texte sur le disque de Phaistos," in *Linguistique balkanique*, 1976, pp. 5–47.

8 Jean Faucounau, *Les Proto-Ioniens. Histoire d'un peuple oublié*, L'Harmattan, Paris 2002; *Les Peuples de la Mer et leur histoire*, L'Harmattan, Paris 2003. See also Alfred Videer, *A l'écoute du disque de Phaistos*, Du Lérot, Tusson 2014.

32

From the Philistines to the Phoenicians

OUT OF ALL OF THE SEA PEOPLES, the most famous one is undoubtedly the Philistines, they are called *Pelischtim* in the Bible where they are mentioned many times. They were settled in Canaan and the Levant, especially in the southern part of the plain along the coastline. They are responsible for its current name, Palestine.[1] The Philistines created a powerful federation of five cities (Gaza, Ashkalon, Ashdod, Ekron and Gath) that became a melting pot and started an original culture. That culture was apparently linked to the Aegean civilization (their painted ceramics are very close to Mycenaean ceramics). Their origins remain controversial. According to a legendary tradition found in the Bible, they come from Caphtor, which has been identified to be Crete. Trude and Moshe Dothan, who underline the kinship between their material culture and the culture of the Mycenaean world, believe that they came from the Aegaen through the intermediary of the Levant. However, the little linguistic and onomastic data we have suggests that they probably came from

---

1 This term is mentioned for the time as *Palastou* in an Assyrian text from 800 BC. "L'histoire biblique, depuis le livre de Josué jusqu'à celui des Chroniques (qui clôt le canon juif), est une alternance de victoires et de défaites des Philistins sur Israël" (Colette Baer, "Palestinien ou Philistin ?," in *Nouveaux Cahiers*, spring 1982, p. 71). See also Jürgen Spanuth, *Die Philister, das unbekannte Volk. Lehrmeister und Widersacher der Israeliter*, Otto Zeller, Osnabrück 1980.

Anatolia. The two theories can coincide if conceding that the Philistines and the Pelasgians described by Herodotus and Thucydides were the "native" inhabitants of Greece. This theory was brought up by the Frenchman Etienne Fourmant in 1747, then by the Egyptologist François Chabas in 1873, and then it was picked up by Vladimir Georgiev, starting from 1950, on the basis of the former Greek denomination of the Pelasgians, *Pelastoi*. Finally, it was more recently picked up with new arguments by Christopher Wilhelm.[2] But "Illyrian" origins were also attributed to the Philistines.[3] Nancy K. Sandars writes that "the Philistines may have only been a ruling class that was absorbed by the local population. In any case, there was something genuinely Nordic in their creation."[4]

We hardly know anything about the Philistine language, beside that it was most likely an Indo-European language, probably close to Luwian or maybe neo-Hittite. As early as the beginning of the 20th century, the Irish archaeologist Robert Alexander Stewart Macalister presented the Philistines as the inventors of the alphabet, and he thought that they shared it with the other Semitic people of Canaan.[5] The searches conducted in the ancient cities of Ashdod, Ashkelon and more importantly Ekron (Tell Mikne) give us reasons to believe that there was a Philistine writing. Some searchers think one example is the four terra cotta tablets found in 1964 by the

---

2 Christopher Wilhelm, "On the Possible Origin of the Philistines," in Karlene Jones-Bley, Martin E. Huld and Angela Della Volpe (ed.), *Proceedings of the Eleventh Annual UCLA Indo-European Conference. Los Angeles, June 4–5, 1999*, Institute for the Study of Man, Washington 2000, pp. 173–182.

3 Indeed, the name Philistines comprises "both an *-ino* suffix which applies to many ethnic groups in ancient Illyricum, and a stem found in the name of the city Palaistè in Epirus," writes Bernard Sergent. He adds the following: "all the regions where both *-ino* and *-st-ino-* can be found coincide fairly well with the now noticeable expansion of languages from the macro-Italic group (Italy, Sicily, Veneto, Istria, Dalmatia). This somewhat makes a case to consider the Philistines to be a people from that group, so, paradoxically, to consider them to be 'Italic'" (*Les Indo-Européens*, op. cit., p. 107–108).

4 *Les Peuples de la Mer*, op. cit., p. 176. See also Trude Dothan, *The Philistines and their Material Culture*, Yale University Press, New Haven 1982; Trude and Moshe Dothan, *Peoples of the Sea. The Search for the Philistines*, Macmillan, New York 1992.

5 Robert Alexander Stewart Macalister, *The Philistines. Their History and Civilization*, British Academy, London 1914, pp. 121–130; *A History of Civilization in Palestine*, Cambridge University Press, Cambridge 1921, p. 33.

Dutch archaeologist Hendricus Jacobus Franken in Tell Deir 'Alla, in the Jordan Valley, but this interpretation remains controversial. The searches in Ashdod also yielded two stratified seals bearing cryptic signs similar to Cypro-Mycenaean writing from the early Bronze Age. They have yet to be deciphered.[6] In August 1976, a five-line inscription on a piece of an earthenware jar (whose fifth line could be an alphabet primer that corresponds beside two exceptions to the twenty-two letters of the Phoenician alphabet) was found inside a silo in Izbet Sartah, in Israel. It dates to the 12th century BC, and it seems to go back to Philistine occupation. Incidentally, the village of Izbet Sartah is only a few kilometers away from the ancient Philistine city of Apheq, where the Philistines won a decisive victory against the Israelites. Nonetheless, the exact origin of the inscription, which has yet to be deciphered, remains controversial.[7] Still, the theory that the Phoenicians got their writing from the Philistines, which lived on the coasts of the Levant before them, must be considered.

The Phoenicians appeared after the invasion of the Sea Peoples, around 1180 BC. In the Iron Age, their territory stretched all across the coastal area of Lebanon, between Mount Casius in the north and Haifa in the south. Their main cities were the city-states of Ugarit, Tyre, Sidon, Akka, Berit and Byblos. The name given to them by the Greeks (*Phoinikes*, from *phoinix*, "red" in Greek) -a name with an Indo-European origin, both from its stem *phoinos*, which is an adjective that means "blood red," and from its suffix *ik* — might have evoked the purple dye that was their specialty. The country they settled in was already inhabited since the 3rd millennium BC by sedentary Canaanite tribes. They quickly mingled with those tribes that might have had Amorite origins. Intentionally focused on the sea, they quickly established a real maritime empire that comprised many trading posts. Their ships had horse heads as figureheads. Their pilots could find their way

---

6   See Hendricus Jacobus Franken, "Clay Tablets from Deir 'Alla, Jordan," in Vetus Testamentum, 1964, pp. 377–379; André Lemaire, "Deux tablettes non déchiffrées de Deir 'Alla," in Fawzi Zayadine and al. (ed.), *La voie royale, 9000 ans d'art au royaume de Jordanie*, Association française d'action artistique, Paris 1986, p. 85.

7   See Joseph Naveh, "Some Considerations on the Ostracon from 'Izbet Sartah," in *Israel Exploration Journal*, 1978, pp. 31–35. See also Trude Dothan, "La première apparition de l'écriture en Philistie," in Rina Viers (ed.), *Des signes pictographiques à l'alphabet*, op. cit., pp. 165–171.

Ursa Minor. They founded Carthage in 814 BC. Phoenicia was added to the Roman province of Syria in 64 BC.

The Phoenician language belongs to the Canaanite language group (west Semitic), but the origin of the Phoenician people is still unknown. According to Gerhard Herm, who believes their ancestors were from a region located between Western Europe and Southern Russia, the Phoenicians sprung out of a fusion between Canaanites and Sea Peoples settled on the coasts of the Levant, in particular the Philistines and the Sakars. He writes that the Sea Peoples "had to unite with the Canaanites later on and be absorbed by them. This fusion, gave birth to the Phoenician nation, whose maritime knowledge was built on the Sea Peoples' expertise."[8] Then the Phoenicians supposedly shared the art of high sea navigation and maybe iron metallurgy to Semitic people. The Hebrews also asked their help to build the Temple in Jerusalem, according to what is written in the Bible.[9] Gerhard Herm adds that "the formula Canaanites + Sea Peoples = Phoenicians cannot be questioned." The great specialist on this topic Sabatino Moscati agrees.[10]

So, it seems reasonable to claim that the Sea Peoples had a system of symbols that were the source of the Phoenician alphabet, but also other Mediterranean writings and maybe the Libyco-Berber script called *tifinagh* in Tuareg.[11] This theory doesn't dismiss the influence that those writing systems had on each other, but it suggests a common heritage. It explains the formal similarities between the Phoenician, Greek, Etruscan, Latin and Germanic (runic) writings without having to make them derive from one another.

---

8   *Les Phéniciens*, op. cit., p. 66.

9   Letter of Salomon to Hiram, king of Tyre (1 Kings 5, 17-20). The Phoenicians, who are sometimes called "Sidonians" in the Bible, are also the people who created the first copper mine in the Gulf of Aqaba. During David's reign, the Hebrew bought large amounts of ore and cedar trunks from them (1 Chronicles 22, 3-4). Relations got worse after the marriage of the eldest son of the king of Israel, Achab, with the daughter of the king of Tyre, Jezabel. She was assassinated, and this led to the massacre of the royal family of Israel and of the princes of Judea (2 Kings 9-10). Lastly, the temple of Baal was destroyed and its priests massacred (2 Chronicles 23, 17).

10 Sabatino Moscati, *The World of the Phoenicians*, Praeger, New York 1968 (French translation: *L'épopée des Phéniciens*, Fayard, Paris 1971).

11 On the debate on the origins of this writing, see Dominique Casajus, *L'alphabet touareg*, CNRS Éditions, Paris 2015.

33

The Etruscans

AMONG THE AUTHORS OF Antiquity, only Dionysius of Halicarnassus (I, 30) wrote that the Etruscans were natives of Italy. All the other authors, Strabo, Plutarch, Livy, Virgil, Horace, Ovid, Tacitus, and Seneca the Younger sided with Herodotus in saying that they came from Asia minor. The theory that the Etruscans were natives of Italy and were descendants of Villanovians or Apenninians was picked up in 1926 by the Italian archaeologist Massimo Pallottino. This theory is heavily criticized nowadays. Everything suggests that the Etruscans do come from Asia minor, as it is written in Virgil's *Aeneid*, as well as in other ancient texts.

Christopher Wilhelm does not shy away from connecting the Etruscans with the dispersion of the Sea Peoples at the end of the Bronze Age,[1] but there is every reason to believe that their ancestors already occupied in the 14th century BC some of the Troad, in north-western Anatolia. That is because Hittite archives mention at that time a Tyrrhenian country west of them. After having taken part in the Sea Peoples' offensive against Egypt, they supposedly settled in Crete, the island of Lemnos and in the Aegean Islands. Then they supposedly mass migrated to northeastern Italy at the same time

---

1 Christopher Wilhelm, "The 'Aeneid' and Italian Prehistory," in Stephanie W. Jamison, H. Craig Melchert and Brent Wine (ed.), *Proceedings of the 22nd Annual UCLA Indo-European Conference. Los Angeles, November 5th and 6th, 2010*, Hempen, Bremen 2011, pp. 255–268. See also Norbert Oettinger, "Seevölker und Etrusker," in Yoram Cohen, Amir Gilan and Jared L. Miller (ed.), *Pax Hethitica. Studies on the Hittites and their Neighbours in Honour of Itamar Singer*, Otto Harrassowitz, Wiesbaden 2010.

as the future Rhaetic populations, which may have been driven out of Asia minor by the arrival of the Phrygians. Thucydides (IV, 109) also thought that they were related to the Pelasgians. Hellanicus of Lesbos, another Greek historian, thought that they were Pelasgians that landed at the mouth of the Po, in northern Italy. As we've seen earlier in this book, Egyptians from the Ramesses III period knew them under the name Teresh (*trsh*) or Tursha, which corresponds to the Latin name *Tusci* derived from **Turschi*. Called Tursānes or Tyrsenians (*Tursēnoi*) by the Greeks, they were called Tyrrhenians afterwards. Later on, the Umbri and the Latins called them the Etruscans. The name *E-trus-cī* is derived from the ancient forms **Trōs-es* and **Trōs-yā*, which confirms that the Trojans and the Etruscans were related. Fritz Schachermeyr also believed that the Etruscans came from a territory in northwestern Asia minor that comprised the Troad, Mysia and northern Lydia.[2] The same theory was recently picked up by Robert S. P. Beekes.[3]

This is the ancient migration narrated by the *Aeneid* with the tale of Aeneas, his father Anchises, and also Antenor that was said to have founded the city of Patavium, which is now Padua.[4] So then the Trojan tale told by Virgil would therefore not be a poetic fabrication. The Tyrsenians supposedly lived a long time close to the Lydians, and the latter's vocabulary eased its way into the former's language (the Lydian name Srkastu seems to correspond to Sergestus, a companion of Aeneas in the Aeneid). Beekes also believes that the name of Ascanius, Aeneas's son, is related to an ally of the Trojans named Askanios in the Iliad. By the way, the Aeneid is not the only ancient text that mentions that the future Etruscans left for Italy. Another tale mentions an Etruscan migration led by Cory(n)thos, son of Paris and Oenone, and the Etruscan city of Tarquinia (founded by a legendary hero that might have been assimilated with the Anatolia god of storms Tarhuntas) is also known as Corythus or Corinthus. Two centuries before

---

2   Fritz Schachermeyr, *Etruskische Frühgeschichte*, Walter de Gruyter, Berlin 1929.

3   Robert S. P. Beekes, *The Origin of the Etruscans*, Koninklijke Nederlands Akademie van Wetenschappen, Amsterdam 2003.

4   Livy describes Antenor as the chief of the Eneti mentioned in the *Iliad* (II, 852), whose name has sometimes been linked to the name of the Veneti. The center of his cult was located in Aponus, which is now Abano, near Padua. See Lorenzo Braccesi, *La leggenda di Antenore. Da Troia a Padova*, Signum, Padova 1984.

Virgil, Gnaeus Naevius described the Aeneas's journey from Troy to Italy in the prologue of his *Bellum Punicum*. Moreover, the oldest representation of the escape from Troy that we know of is on an Etruscan vase from the 7th century BC.

It was believed for a long time that the Etruscans arrived in Italy only in the 8th century BC because they appear on the map at that time, on a territory between the Arno and the Tiber. But Herodotus, who describes the Tyrrhenians as Lydians that left their land under the direction of the legendary king Tyrrhenus, son of Atys, assures us that they settled in the Italian peninsula much earlier. We know that there had been relations between the Mycenaean kingdom of Pylos and the Tyrrhenian coast, north of Latium, as early as the third quarter of the 2nd millennium BC. So, the historical Etruscans were supposedly the result of the fusion of newcomers and the native population made of Villanovians and Apenninians.

The Anatolian origin of the Etruscans has finally been confirmed by genetics. Studies on the mitochondrial DNA of Tuscan people have confirmed that they are related with populations from Anatolia.[5]

The Estruscan language is generally not considered part of the Indo-European language group. We know how to read it but we still don't know how to decipher it. Still, some linguists affirm that they are related to the Indo-European languages of Anatolia. They argue that those languages are quite original compared to Proto-Indo-European. Vladimir Georgiev, who makes it out to be the heir of Hittite, believes that the language was derived from a Luwian dialect related to Lydian.[6] Francisco Adrados also thinks that it is related to Luwian, whereas Jean Faucounau links Etruscan to Lycian. Giulio Facchetti thinks he can make a connection between Proto-Tyrsenian, the ancestor of the Etruscan language, and Minoan documents written in Linear A.[7] Paul Kretschmer thinks there is a connection between

---

5   See Cristiano Vernesi, David Caramelli, Isabelle Dupanloup et al., "The Etruscans: A Population-Genetic Study," in *American Journal of Human Genetics*, 2004, pp. 694–704.

6   Vladimir Georgiev, *La lingua e l'origine degli Etruschi*, Nagard, Roma 1979; "L'origine degli Etruschi come problema della storia delle tribù egee," in *Studi etruschi*, 1950, pp. 101–124.

7   Giulio Facchetti, *Appunti di morfologia etrusca. Con un appendice sulla questione delle affinità genetiche dell'etrusco*, S. Olschki, Firenze 2002.

languages like Rhaetian, Lycian, Etruscan and "Proto-Indo-European" populations.[8] More recently, Fred C. Woudhuizen attempted to decipher the longest known Etruscan text using Luwian.[9] All those attempts to find connections remain uncertain. It is certain that there Etruscan has an Anatolian component (the name of the Tarquinia most likely reflects the stem of the Hittite verb *tarh-* "vanquish" and in particular its derivations with *-u-*). But trying to make it an Anatolian language stumbles over the fact that the more conservative sectors of the vocabulary like the numerals and the names of relatives can not be interpreted from the perspective of Anatolian languages. Finally, it should be noted that the language spoken in Sardinia before the Romanization may have been related to Etruscan, but it may not have necessarily been derived from it.[10]

The fact that the Etruscans were not natives of Italy raises the question as to how they came to see the alphabet. Was it handed to them by the Greeks, like how it is generally believed, or was it handed to them by the Phoenicians? After they settled in Italy or before? Did they bring to Italy an alphabet derived from the same source the Phoenician alphabet is derived from? Was there a lineage or a parallel evolution?

The Etruscan alphabet is present on many objects. The oldest one was discovered in the princely tomb of Marsiliana d'Albegna, and dates to around 700 BC. This alphabet comprises twenty-six letters, most of them are very similar to Greek letters. It also comprises signs that show no resemblance to Phoenician or classical Greek. This alphabet seems to come from Cumae, a former Greek colony near Naples. Since this alphabet (whose number of letters was later reduced to twenty) is almost contemporary of the more ancient known Etruscan inscriptions, the inscriptions of the great

---

8   On the question of the relationship between Etruscan and Rhaetian languages, see Helmut Rix, *Rätisch und Etruskisch*, Institut für Sprachwissenschaft der Universität Innsbruck, Innsbruck 1998.

9   Fred C. Woudhuizen, *The Liber Linteus. A Word for Word Commentary to and Translation of the Longest Etruscan Text*, Innsbrucker Beiträge zur Kulturwissenschaft, Innsbruck 2013. From the same author, see also *Etruscan as a Colonial Luwian Language*, Institut für Sprachen und Literaturen der Universität Innsbruck, Innsbruck 2008; "Etruscan and Luwian," in *The Journal of Indo-European Studies*, 1991, pp. 133–150.

10 See Massimo Pittau, *La lingua sardiana o dei Protosardi*, Ettore Gasperini, Cagliari 2001.

necropolises of Tarquinia (Monterozzi) and Banditaccia (Cerveteri), we positively know that it was written from right to left or in boustrophedon mode. But what Greek alphabet was it derived from? The first version of the Greek system used by the Etruscans was supposedly the archaic Greek alphabet used in the town of Chalcis in Euboea, at the end of the 8th century BC. After having been brought by the Greeks that came to Ischia to settle, it was then supposedly transmitted to the Chalcidian colony that founded around the −760 the town of Cumae. This Chalcidian alphabet also supposedly influenced the Sicels' alphabet (Sicily) and the Messapian alphabet (Apulia and Calabria). According to another tradition passed on by Pliny, it was the Pelasgians that created the Italic alphabets.

However, Albert Grenier thought that the "Hellenic character" of Etruscan writing could have been present before the Greek colonization of Southern Italy. The 1885 discovery of two funeral steles near Kaminia, on the island of Lemnos and facing the coasts of Asia minor, that bear inscriptions written in a Greek alphabet, but in a language close to Etruscan ("etruscoid") rekindled the debate.[11] Marcel Cohen writes that

> the strokes definitely give the impression that the Etruscan alphabet is related to Greek, [but the characters] give the impression that they are relics of an ancient writing from another system.[12]

Since Lemnos was Hellenized only 150 years later, those steles were probably made by Tyrsenians from the north of the Aegean Sea. So,

> the spawning of the Etruscan civilization in Tuscany, in the 8th century BC, would therefore be the result of a long presence (four centuries) during which Tyrsenian warriors of Etruria, mercenaries or conquerors, progressively established their domination over the country.[13]

---

11 See Carlo De Simone, *I Tirreni a Lemnos. Evidenze linguistica e tradizioni storiche*, S. Olschki, Firenze 1996.

12 Marcel Cohen, *La grande invention de l'écriture et son évolution*, C. Klincksieck, Paris 1958. See also Roger Druet and Herman Grégoire, *La civilisation de l'écriture*, Fayard, Paris 1970, p. 33.

13 "Mais d'où viennent les Etrusques?," in *L'Histoire*, September 1994, p. 67.

34

From Etruscan to Latin

IT IS GENERALLY BELIEVED that the 8th century is the earliest possible date for the creation of the Latin alphabet. Indeed, the oldest Latin inscriptions don't go back further than the end of the 7th century. It is notably the case for the Lapis Niger found in 1899 on a stele of the Roman Forum, which could date to the 6th century, and for the Etruscan-made golden fibula found in Palestrina, in southern Lazio, that dates to around 600 BC. But there's few Latin inscriptions that go further back than the 1st century BC. "This writing was originally used for religious and magical purposes," writes Raymond Bloch, who adds that "this writing was easily thought to have a divine origin."[1]

The Romans supposedly got their writing (that originally only comprised twenty letters) from the Etruscans, after a few modifications done by the Tuscans. The populations in the south of the peninsula (the Messapians in Apulia and Calabria, the Osci in Lucania and Messina) got it straight from the Greeks. If the Latin people were directly inspired by the Greeks, they would actually have had graphemes that could have helped them distinguish the voiced occlusive velar /g/ from the voiceless one /k/. The fact that in the earlier inscriptions, those two value were represented by C seems to indicate that their model wasn't the Greek alphabet, but the Etruscan alphabet in which those two values are not differentiated. This theory, which

---

[1] Raymond Bloch, "Quand les Romains apprenaient à lire et à écrire," in *L'Histoire*, January 1982, p. 12.

is the more popular one, remains controversial nonetheless. Indeed, the Etruscan alphabet doesn't use the letters o, b and d, which casts doubt on the likelihood of the borrowing. The Roman alphabet was then expanded in the 3rd century BC by adding the letter G. This letter was created by adding a stroke to C. It was further expanded in the 1st century BC by adding the letters Y and Z. They were added to make transcribing from Greek easier. So, in the classical period, the Latin alphabet had twenty-three letters.

However, the literacy rate of the Roman population in of the 1st century AD supposedly peaked at 20 %.[2]

---

[2] See William V. Harris, Ancient Literacy, Harvard University Press, Cambridge 1989; Christoph Bernhard Rüger, "Lateinische Schriflichkeit im römischen Grenzgebiet gegen die Germanen," in *Runeninschriften als Quellen interdisziplinärer Forschung*, op. cit., pp. 357–375.

THE MÖJEBRO RUNESTONE (Uppland), illustrated by a horse rider brandishing a sword. The inscription "FrawaradaR anahaha is larginaR" is written from right to left.

THE JÄRVSTA RUNESTONE (Sweden), dating to the 11th century.
It evokes the memory of a king named Þjóðmundr.

INDEX

A

Adam of Bremen 90, 109

Aegean 67, 142–160

Æsir 63–70, 112

Ættir x, 7–17, 44–45, 61–63, 79–82, 98, 123

A

Africanus, Sextus Julius 62

Alani 82

Alraun 78

Altamira 66

Antonsen, Elmer H. 12, 26–48, 71–77

Arntz, Helmut 34–37, 63, 81–85

Askeberg, Fritz 24–25

B

Baltic Sea 30

Bede 102

Beowulf 77

Berserkir 90

Black Sea 29–31, 46–47, 85

Bracteate 57

Brahmin 2

Brandeburg tomb 13

Bugge, Sophus 7, 29–31, 47, 70, 85

C

Carinthia 32–34

Celts 2, 23, 90, 103–120

Cicero 82

Cimbri 35–46, 82

Coligny calendar 103

D

Denmark 5–13, 25, 44–50, 83–100, 129

Derolez, René 5–19, 72–79, 109

Dillman, François-Xavier 20–27, 69

Düwel, Klaus 12–43, 64–75

E

Egill's Saga 92

F

Fibula 7–14, 39, 85, 130, 161

Fortunatus, Venantius 18

Freyja 70

Fuþark, Old 5–12, 38–45, 74–84

Fuþark, Young 21

Fuþorc, Anglo-Saxon 5–9, 48

G

Gematria 62

Golden Horns of Gallehus 10, 31, 129

Goths 25–47, 78, 128

Greek 2–48, 62, 76–85, 101–162

Grettir's Saga 92

H

Hagia Triada 142

Hammarström, Magnus 33–34, 47

Hávamál 87–91, 108, 122

Herodotus 81, 133, 153–158

Herodotus 81, 133, 153–158

Hickes, John 9

Høst, Gerd 72, 85

Hyksos 141–142

I

Illyrian (dialect) 32–34, 153

Indo-Europeans 17, 67, 101–121, 142

Italic 32–48, 64, 82–86, 153–160

J

Jarl 86

K

Kovel spearhead 13

Krause, Wolfgang 8–46, 60–85, 119

L

Latin 3–48, 61–115, 155–162

Lepontii alphabet 33

Lex Frisionum 83

Linear A (script) 142–158

M

Marez, Alain 37, 60–61, 73–84

Mas d'Azil 66

Medinet Haby 149–151

Merovingians 18

Mesopotamia 68, 141–148

Minoans 142

Moisson, Patrick 69

Moltke, Erik 25–27, 40–45, 71–85

Monotheism 69

Moon 98–105, 123

Musset, Lucien 8–47, 60–87

N

Neckel, Gustav 22, 63

Neolithic 67, 99–101

Nordic Bronze Age 65, 125

North Etruscan 20–22, 35–36

O

Óðhinn 11

Ogham 23–33, 49

Ogmios 24, 90

Orpheus 134

P

Page, Raymond I. 18–20, 71

Parsons, David N. 48, 60

Phaistos Disk 150–151

Philistines 149–155

Phoenicians 133–159

Pliny the Elder 81, 102

Plutarch 3, 81–82, 156

Poetic Edda 76–105

Proto-Germanic 41, 76, 138

Proto-Nordic 41, 85
Proto-Sinaitic 141–146

R

Rhineland 25, 62
Roman 13–41, 62–64, 79–85, 103–112, 155–162
Runesmith 92
Rupestrian 35, 65

S

Sanskrit 2
Scythians 81
Siculus, Diodorus 98, 133–134
Skald 88–93
Sorcery 70–78
Stafr 17
Sumerian 67–68, 140–141

T

Tacitus 25, 78–82, 101–102, 116, 133, 156
Teutons 46

U

Upper Paleolithic 66, 99–100

V

Val Camonica 35–36, 65–66
Valkyries 122
Vanir 63–70
Varuna 90
Vedic 2, 86, 99, 115–121
Venus of Laussel 99
Völuspá 111–112
von Friesen, Otto 29–30, 46–47

W

Watzinger, Carl 141
Wimmer, Ludwig F.A. 4–23, 47

Y

Yggdrasill 108–112

Z

Zodiac 121

OTHER BOOKS PUBLISHED BY ARKTOS

Sri Dharma Pravartaka Acharya	*The Dharma Manifesto*
Joakim Andersen	*Rising from the Ruins: The Right of the 21st Century*
Alain de Benoist	*Beyond Human Rights*
	Carl Schmitt Today
	The Indo-Europeans
	Manifesto for a European Renaissance
	On the Brink of the Abyss
	The Problem of Democracy
	View from the Right (vol. 1–3)
Arthur Moeller van den Bruck	*Germany's Third Empire*
Matt Battaglioli	*The Consequences of Equality*
Kerry Bolton	*Revolution from Above*
	Yockey: A Fascist Odyssey
Isac Boman	*Money Power*
Ricardo Duchesne	*Faustian Man in a Multicultural Age*
Alexander Dugin	*Ethnos and Society*
	Eurasian Mission: An Introduction to Neo-Eurasianism
	The Fourth Political Theory
	Last War of the World-Island
	Putin vs Putin
	The Rise of the Fourth Political Theory
Koenraad Elst	*Return of the Swastika*
Julius Evola	*The Bow and the Club*
	Fascism Viewed from the Right
	A Handbook for Right-Wing Youth
	Metaphysics of War
	Notes on the Third Reich
	The Path of Cinnabar
	Recognitions
	A Traditionalist Confronts Fascism

OTHER BOOKS PUBLISHED BY ARKTOS

GUILLAUME FAYE	*Archeofuturism*
	Archeofuturism 2.0
	The Colonisation of Europe
	Convergence of Catastrophes
	A Global Coup
	Sex and Deviance
	Understanding Islam
	Why We Fight
DANIEL S. FORREST	*Suprahumanism*
ANDREW FRASER	*Dissident Dispatches*
	The WASP Question
GÉNÉRATION IDENTITAIRE	*We are Generation Identity*
PAUL GOTTFRIED	*War and Democracy*
PORUS HOMI HAVEWALA	*The Saga of the Aryan Race*
RACHEL HAYWIRE	*The New Reaction*
LARS HOLGER HOLM	*Hiding in Broad Daylight*
	Homo Maximus
	Incidents of Travel in Latin America
	The Owls of Afrasiab
ALEXANDER JACOB	*De Naturae Natura*
JASON REZA JORJANI	*Prometheus and Atlas*
	World State of Emergency
RODERICK KAINE	*Smart and SeXy*
LANCE KENNEDY	*Supranational Union and New Medievalism*
PETER KING	*Here and Now*
	Keeping Things Close
LUDWIG KLAGES	*The Biocentric Worldview*
	Cosmogonic Reflections
PIERRE KREBS	*Fighting for the Essence*

OTHER BOOKS PUBLISHED BY ARKTOS

STEPHEN PAX LEONARD	*Travels in Cultural Nihilism*
PENTTI LINKOLA	*Can Life Prevail?*
H. P. LOVECRAFT	*The Conservative*
CHARLES MAURRAS	*The Future of the Intelligentsia & For a French Awakening*
MICHAEL O'MEARA	*Guillaume Faye and the Battle of Europe*
	New Culture, New Right
BRIAN ANSE PATRICK	*The NRA and the Media*
	Rise of the Anti-Media
	The Ten Commandments of Propaganda
	Zombology
TITO PERDUE	*The Bent Pyramid*
	Morning Crafts
	Philip
	William's House (vol. 1–4)
RAIDO	*A Handbook of Traditional Living*
STEVEN J. ROSEN	*The Agni and the Ecstasy*
	The Jedi in the Lotus
RICHARD RUDGLEY	*Barbarians*
	Essential Substances
	Wildest Dreams
ERNST VON SALOMON	*It Cannot Be Stormed*
	The Outlaws
SRI SRI RAVI SHANKAR	*Celebrating Silence*
	Know Your Child
	Management Mantras
	Patanjali Yoga Sutras
	Secrets of Relationships
GEORGE T. SHAW	*A Fair Hearing: The Alt-Right in the Words of Its Members and Leaders*

OTHER BOOKS PUBLISHED BY ARKTOS

OSWALD SPENGLER	*Man and Technics*
TOMISLAV SUNIC	*Against Democracy and Equality*
	Postmortem Report
	Titans are in Town
HANS-JÜRGEN SYBERBERG	*On the Fortunes and Misfortunes of Art in Post-War Germany*
ABIR TAHA	*Defining Terrorism: The End of Double Standards*
	The Epic of Arya (2nd ed.)
	Nietzsche's Coming God, or the Redemption of the Divine
	Verses of Light
BAL GANGADHAR TILAK	*The Arctic Home in the Vedas*
DOMINIQUE VENNER	*For a Positive Critique*
	The Shock of History
MARKUS WILLINGER	*A Europe of Nations*
	Generation Identity

CPSIA information can be obtained
at www.ICGtesting.com
Printed in the USA
BVHW031624250321
603414BV00001B/62